John Pentland Mahaffy

Old Greek Education

John Pentland Mahaffy

Old Greek Education

ISBN/EAN: 9783743320307

Manufactured in Europe, USA, Canada, Australia, Japa

Cover: Foto ©ninafisch / pixelio.de

Manufactured and distributed by brebook publishing software (www.brebook.com)

John Pentland Mahaffy

Old Greek Education

OLD GREEK EDUCATION

BY

J. P. MAHAFFY, M.A.

FELL. AND TUTOR, TRIN. COLL., DUB.
KNIGHT OF THE ORDER OF THE SAVIOUR
AUTHOR OF 'SOCIAL LIFE IN GREECE' 'A HISTORY OF GREEK LITERATURE'
'A PRIMER OF GREEK ANTIQUITIES' ETC.

LONDON
KEGAN PAUL, TRENCH, & CO., 1, PATERNOSTER SQUARE
1881

(The rights of translation and of reproduction are reserved)

TO THE

GREEK NATION

STILL, AS OF OLD, THE PIONEER OF EDUCATION

IN EASTERN EUROPE

I DEDICATE

THIS LITTLE BOOK

IN MEMORY OF THE YEAR 1881

PREFATORY NOTE.

READERS unfamiliar with Greek will find the equivalent of the Greek words cited in the nearest word printed in italics.

The scope of this book precludes me from acknowledging individually my many obligations to other authors, both for curious facts and for learned references.

CONTENTS.

CHAPTER		PAGE
	INTRODUCTION	1
I.	INFANCY	9
II.	EARLIER CHILDHOOD	16
III.	SCHOOL DAYS—THE PHYSICAL SIDE	24
IV.	SCHOOL DAYS—THE MUSICAL SIDE—THE SCHOOLMASTER	37
V.	THE MUSICAL SIDE—SCHOOLS AND THEIR APPOINTMENTS	48
VI.	THE SUBJECTS AND METHOD OF EDUCATION—DRAWING AND MUSIC.	65
VII.	THE LAST STAGE OF EDUCATION—MILITARY TRAINING OF THE EPHEBI	78
VIII.	HIGHER EDUCATION—THE SOPHISTS AND SOCRATES	88
IX.	THE RHETORS—ISOCRATES	103
X.	THE GREEK THEORISTS ON EDUCATION—PLATO AND ARISTOTLE	112
XI.	THE GROWTH OF SYSTEMATIC HIGHER EDUCATION—UNIVERSITY LIFE AT ATHENS	131
	INDEX	157

GREEK EDUCATION.

INTRODUCTION.

§ 1. WE hear it often repeated that human nature is the same at all times and in all places, and this is urged at times and places where it is so manifestly false, that we feel disposed peremptorily to deny it when paraded to us as a general truth. The fact is that only in its lower activities does human nature show any remarkable uniformity; so far as men are mere animals, they have strong resemblances, and in savages, even their minds seem to originate the same fancies in various ages and climes. But when we come to higher developments, to the spiritual element in individuals, to the social and political relations of civilised men, the pretended truism gives way more and more to the opposite truth, that mankind varies at all times and in all places. As no two individuals, when carefully examined, are exactly alike, so no two societies of men are even nearly alike; and at the present time there is probably no more fertile cause of political and legislative blundering than the assumption that the constitution successfully worked out by one people can be transferred by the force of a mere decree to its neighbours. All the recent experiments in state-reform have been based on this assumption, as if the transference of a House of Commons in any real sense were not as impossible as the transference of Eton and of Oxford to some foreign society.

Although, therefore, we cannot deny that past history contains many fruitful lessons for the bettering of our own time, it is not unlikely that the tendency of the present widely informed, but hasty, age is to exaggerate the likenesses of various epochs, and to overrate the force of analogy in social and political reasoning. Historical parallels are generally striking only up to a certain point; a deeper knowledge discloses elements of contrast, wide differences of motive, great variations in human feeling.

§ 2. But as we go back to simpler states of life, or earlier stages of development, the argument from analogy becomes stronger, and the lessons we may derive from history, though less striking, are more trustworthy. This is peculiarly the case with the problem of education, as handled by civilised nations in various ages. The material to be worked upon is that simpler and fresher human nature, in which varieties are due only to heredity, and not yet to the numerous artificial stimulants and restraints which every society of mature men invents for itself. The games and sports of children, all over the world, are as uniform as the weapons and designs of savages. The delights and disappointments of education have also remained the same, at least in many respects.

The conflict of theoretical and practical educators, and the failure of splendid schemes for the reform of society by a systematic training of youth, mark every overripe civilisation. Here then, if anywhere, we may gain a distinct advantage by contemplating the problems, which we ourselves are solving, under discussion in a remote society. The more important and permanent elements will stand out clearer when freed from the interests and prejudices of our own day, and from the necessities of our own situation; and thus we may be taught to regain freedom of judgment and escape from the iron despotism of a traditional system. For if it be the case that in no department of our life are we more thoroughly enslaved than on the question of education, if it be true that we are obliged here to submit our children to the ignorance and prejudice of nurses, governesses, priests, pedants— all following more or less stupid traditions, and all coerced by shackles which they want either the knowledge or the power to break—then any enquiry which may lead us to consider freely and calmly what is right and what is not right, what is possible and what is not possible in education cannot but have real value, apart from purely historical or learned considerations.

§ 3. In fact, the main object of this book is to interest men who are not classical scholars, and who are not professional educators, in the theory of education, as treated by that people which is known to have done more than any other in fitting its members for the higher ends and enjoyments of life. The Greeks were far behind us in the mechanical aids to human progress; they understood not the use of electricity, or of steam, or of gunpowder, or of printing. But, in spite of this, the Greek public was far better educated than we are—nay, to some extent, because of this it was better educated. For Greek life afforded proper leisure for thorough intellectual training, and this includes first of all such political training as is strange to almost the whole of Europe; secondly, moral training of so high a kind as to rival at times the light of revelation; thirdly, social training to something higher than music and feasting by way of recreation; and fourthly, artistic training, which, while it did not condescend to bad imitations of great artists, taught the public to understand and to love true and noble ideals.

Why must these great ends of education be obscured or lost by the modern wonders of discovery, which should make them more easy of attainment and wider in circulation? Were the Greeks better off in education than we are, and if so, why were they better off? or is all this alleged Greek superiority an idle dream of the pedants, with no solid basis in facts? If it is real, can we not discover the secret of their superiority, and use it with far wider and deeper effect in our Christian society? or is human nature of narrow and fixed capacity, and does the addition of wide ranges of positive science and of various tongues mar irrevocably the cultivation of the pure reason and of the æsthetic faculty? These are the problems which will occupy the following pages, not in their abstract form; they will be considered in close relation to the success or failure of the old Greeks in discussing and solving them.

§ 4. There have been only two earlier nations, and one later, which could compete with the Greeks in their treatment of this perpetual problem in human progress. We have first the Egyptian nation, which by its thorough and widely diffused culture attained a duration of national prosperity and happiness perhaps never since equalled. Isolated from other civilised races by geographical position, by language, and in consequence by social institutions, the Egyptians prosecuted internal development more assiduously than is the wont of mere conquering races. The few foreign possessions acquired by the Egyptians were never assimilated, and the civilisation of the Nile remained isolated and unique. We have reason to know that this refined social life, which is perpetuated in pictures on the monuments of the land, this large and various literature, of which so many fragments have been recovered in our century, was not created without a diffused and systematic education. In Plato's *Laws*,[1] the training of their young children in elementary science is described as far superior to anything in Greece. But, unfortunately, the materials for any estimate of Egyptian education, in its process, are wanting. We can see plainly its great national effects; we have even some details as to the special training in separate institutions of a learned and literary class; but nothing more has yet been recovered. If we knew the various steps by which Moses became 'learned in all the wisdom of the Egyptians,' an interesting field of comparison would be opened to us; and here no doubt we should find some of our own difficulties

[1] p. 819.

discussed and perhaps solved by early sages, still more by an enlightened public opinion, showing itself in the establishment of sound traditions. And no doubt from the dense population, the subdivision of property and of labour, and the absence of a great territorial aristocracy, the education of the Egyptians must have corresponded to our middle class and primary systems, together with special institutions for the higher training of the professions and of the literary caste.

§ 5. If we could command our material, we might seek elsewhere for analogies to the education of our nobility and higher gentry. We know through Greek and Roman sources, as well as through the heroic poetry of the *Shahnameh*, that the Aryan nobles who became, under Cyrus, the rulers of Western Asia, were in character, as they were in blood, allied to the Germanic chiefs and Norse Vikings, with their love of daring adventure, their chivalry, and their intense loyalty to their appointed sovereign. In these qualities they were strangely opposed to the democratic Greeks, on whom they looked with contempt, while they were appreciated in return only by a few such men as Herodotus and Xenophon. Indeed, such devotion to their sovereign as made them leap overboard to lighten his ship in a storm was confounded by the Greeks with slavish submission, oriental prostrations, and other signs of humiliation. Nevertheless, the men whom the Greeks long dared not look in the face —the conquerors of half the known world, the successful rivals of the Romans for the dominion of the East— faced death under Xerxes and the last Darius with other feelings than those of slavish submission. Herodotus, in his interesting and sympathetic account of them, says their children's education consisted of three things—to ride, to shoot, and to tell the truth. If he had added a chivalrous loyalty to their kings like that of the French nobles in the last century, he would have completed the picture, and sketched a training which many an English gentleman considers little short of perfection.

§ 6. The Romans are the only other ancient people who stand near enough to us to suggest an enquiry into their education. And it may be said that they combined the dignity of noble traditions with the practical instincts of a successful trading people. Hence Roman education, if carried on with system, ought of all others to correspond with that of Englishmen, who should combine the same qualities in carrying out an analogous policy, and in filling to some extent a similar position in the world. But so closely was all Roman culture based on Greek books and models that, although every people must develop individual features of its own—and the Romans had plenty of them, as we may see from Quintilian—any philosophical knowledge of Roman education must depend upon a previous knowledge of the Greeks. In many respects the Romans were a race more congenial to the English, and hence by us more easily understood. In the coarser and stronger elements of human character, in directness and love of truth, in a certain contempt of æsthetics and of speculation, in a blunt assertion of the supremacy of practical questions, in a want of sympathy, and often a stupid ignorance and neglect of the character and requirements of subject races, the Romans are the true forerunners of the English in history. Burdened as we are with these defects of national character, the products of the subtler and more genial, if less solid and truthful, Hellenic race are particularly well worth our consideration. This has been so thoroughly recognised by thoughtful men in our generation as to require no further support by argument. It only remains that each of our Hellenists should do his best in some distinct line to make the life of the Greeks known to us with fairness and accuracy.

CHAPTER I.

INFANCY.

§ 7. WE find in Homer, especially in the Iliad, indications of the plainest kind that Greek babies were like the babies of modern Europe, equally troublesome, equally delightful to their parents, equally uninteresting to the rest of society. The famous scene in the sixth book of the Iliad, when Hector's infant, Astyanax, screams at the sight of his father's waving crest, and the hero lays his helmet on the ground that he may laugh and weep over the child; the love and tenderness of Andromache, and her pathetic laments in the twenty-second book, are familiar to all. She foresees the hardships and unkindnesses to her orphan boy, 'who was wont upon his father's knees to eat the purest marrow and the rich fat of sheep, and when sleep came upon him, and he ceased his childish play, he would lie in the arms of his nurse, on a soft cushion, satisfied with every comfort.' So again [1] a protecting goddess is compared to a mother keeping the flies from her sleeping infant, and a pertinacious friend [2] to a little girl who, running beside her mother, begs to be taken up, holding her mother's dress and delaying her, and with tearful eyes

---

[1] Δ 130.   [2] Π 7.

keeps looking up till the mother denies her no longer. These are only stray references, and yet they speak no less clearly than if we had asked for an express answer to a direct enquiry. So we have the hesitation of the murderers sent to make away with the infant Cypselus, who had been foretold to portend danger to the Corinthian Herods of that day. The smile of the baby unmans—or should we rather say unbrutes?—the first ruffian, and so the task is passed on from man to man. This story in Herodotus [1] is a sort of natural Greek parallel to the great Shakesperian scene, where another child sways his intended torturer with an eloquence more conscious and explicit, but not perhaps more powerful, than the radiant smile of the Greek baby. Thus Euripides, the great master of pathos, represents Iphigenia bringing her infant brother Orestes to plead for her with that unconsciousness of sorrow which pierces us to the heart more than the most affecting rhetoric. In modern art a little child playing about its dead mother, and waiting with contentment for her awaking, is perhaps the most powerful appeal to human compassion which we are able to conceive.

On the other hand, the troubles of infancy were then as now very great. We do not indeed hear of croup, or teething, or measles, or whooping cough. But these are occasional matters, and count as nothing beside the inexorable tyranny of a sleepless baby. For then as now mothers and nurses had a strong prejudice in favour of carrying about restless children, and so soothing them to

[1] Herod. v. 93.

sleep. The unpractical Plato requires that in his fabulous Republic two or three stout nurses shall be in readiness to carry about each child, because children, like gamecocks, gain spirit and endurance by this treatment! What they really gain is a gigantic power of torturing their mothers. Most children can readily be taught to sleep in a bed or even in an armchair, but an infant once accustomed to being carried about will insist upon it; and so it came that Greek husbands were obliged to relegate their wives to another sleeping room, where the nightly squalling of the furious infant might not disturb the master as well as the mistress of the house. But the Greek gentleman was able to make good his damaged rest by a midday siesta, and so required but little sleep at night. The modern father in northern Europe, with his whole day's work and waking, is therefore in a more disadvantageous position.

Of course very fashionable people kept nurses, and it was the highest tone at Athens to have a Spartan nurse for the infant, just as an English nurse is sought out among foreign noblesse. We are told that these women made the child hardier, that they used less swathing and bandaging, and allowed free play for the limbs; and this, like all the Spartan physical training, was approved of and admired by the rest of the Greek public, though its imitation was never suggested save in the unpractical speculations of Plato.

Whether they also approved of a diet of marrow and mutton suet, which Homer, in the passage just cited, considers the luxury of princes, does not appear. As Homer was the Greek Bible—an inspired book containing perfect wisdom on all things, human and divine—there must have been many orthodox parents who followed his prescription. But we hear no approval or censure of such diet. Possibly marrow may have represented our cod-liver oil in strengthening delicate infants. But as the Homeric men fed far more exclusively on meat than their historical successors, some vegetable substitute, such as olive oil, must have been in use later on. Even within our memory mutton suet boiled in milk was commonly recommended by physicians for the delicacy now treated by cod-liver oil. √The supposed strengthening of children by air and exposure, or by early neglect of their comforts, was as fashionable at Sparta as it is with many modern theorists, and it probably led in both cases to the same result—the extinction of the weak and delicate. These theorists parade the cases of survival of stout children—that is, their exceptional soundness—as the effect of this harsh treatment, and so satisfy themselves that experience confirms their views. Now with the Spartans this was logical enough, for as they professed and desired nothing but physical results, as they despised intellectual qualities, and esteemed obedience to be the highest of moral ones, they were perhaps justified in their proceeding. So thoroughly did they advocate the production of healthy citizens for military purposes that they were quite content that the sickly should die. In fact, in the case of obviously weak and deformed infants, they did not hesitate to expose them in the most brutal sense, not to cold and draughts, but to the wild beasts in the mountains.

§ 8. This brings us to the first shocking contrast between the Greek treatment of children and ours. We cannot really doubt, from the free use of the idea in Greek tragedies, in the comedies of ordinary life, and in theories of political economy, that the exposing of new-born children was not only sanctioned by public feeling, but actually practised throughout Greece. Various motives combined to justify or to extenuate this practice. In the first place, the infant was regarded as the property of its parents, indeed of its father, to an extent inconceivable to most modern Europeans. The State only, whose claim overrode all other considerations, had a right, for public reasons, to interfere with the dispositions of a father. Individual human life had not attained what may be called the exaggerated value derived from sundry superstitions, which remains even after those superstitions have decayed. And, moreover, in many Greek states, the contempt for commercial pursuits, and the want of outlet for practical energy, made the supporting of large families cumbersome, or the subdivision of patrimonies excessive. Hence the prudence or the selfishness of parents did not hesitate to use an escape which modern civilisation condemns as not only criminal but as horribly cruel. How little even the noblest Greek theorists felt this objection appears from the fact that Plato, the Attic Moses, sanctions infanticide[1] under certain circumstances

---

[1] Exposing children instead of killing them left open the chance that some benevolent person would save them from pity, or avaricious person to sell them as slaves—a result which no doubt often occurred. Thus the parents could console their consciences with a hope that the benevolence of the gods had prevented the natural consequences of their inhuman act.

or in another form, in his ideal state. In the genteel comedy it is often mentioned as a somewhat painful necessity, but enjoined by prudence. Nowhere does the agony of the mother's heart reach us through their literature, save in one illustration used by the Platonic Socrates, where he compares the anger of his pupils, when first confuted out of their prejudices, to the fury of a young mother deprived of her first infant. There is something horrible in the very allusion, as if in after life Attic mothers became hardened to this treatment. We must suppose the exposing of female infants to have been not uncommon until the just retribution of barrenness fell upon the nation, and the population dwindled away by a strange atrophy.

§ 9. In the many family suits argued by the Attic orators we do not (I believe) find a case in which a large family of children is concerned. Four appears a larger number than the average. Marriages between relations as close as uncle and niece, and even half-brothers and sisters, were not uncommon, but the researches of modern science have removed the grounds for believing that this practice would tend to diminish the race. It would certainly increase any *pre-existing* tendency to hereditary disease; yet we do not hear of infantile diseases any more than we hear of delicate infants. Plagues and epidemics were common enough, but, as already observed, we do not hear of measles, or whooping cough, or scarlatina, or any of the other constant persecutors of our nurseries.

As the learning of foreign languages was quite beneath the notions of the Greek gentleman, who rather expected all barbarians to learn *his* language, the habit of employing foreign nurses, so useful and even necessary to good modern education, was well-nigh unknown. It would have been thought a great misfortune to any Hellenic child to be brought up speaking Thracian or Egyptian. Accordingly foreign slave attendants, with their strange accent and rude manners, were not allowed to take charge of children till they were able to go to school, and had learned their mother tongue perfectly.

But the women's apartments, in which children were kept for the first few years, are closed so completely to us that we can but conjecture a few things about the life and care of Greek babies. A few late epigrams tell the grief of parents bereaved of their infants. Beyond this, classical literature affords us no light. The backwardness in culture of Greek women leads us to suspect that then, as now, Greek babies were more often spoilt than is the case among the serious northern nations. The term 'Spartan mother' is, however, still proverbial, and no doubt in that exceptional State discipline was so universal and so highly esteemed that it penetrated even to the nursery. But in the rest of Greece we may conceive the young child arriving at his schoolboy age more wilful and headstrong than most of our more watched and worried infants. Archytas, the philosopher, earned special credit for inventing the rattle, and saving much damage to household furniture by occupying children with this toy.

CHAPTER II.

EARLIER CHILDHOOD.

§ 10. THE external circumstances determining a Greek boy's education were somewhat different from ours. We must remember that all old Greek life, except in rare cases, such as that of Elis, of which we know nothing, was distinctly *town life*, and so naturally Greek schooling was day schooling, from which the children returned to the care of their parents. To hand over boys, far less girls, to the charge of a boarding-school was perfectly unknown, and would no doubt have been gravely censured. Orphans were placed under the care of their nearest male relative, even when their education was provided (as it was in some cases) by the State. Again, as regards the age of going to school, it would naturally be early, seeing that day schools may well include infants of tender age, and that in Greek households neither father nor mother was often able or disposed to undertake the education of the children. Indeed, we find it universal that even the knowledge of the letters, and reading, were obtained from a school-master. All these circumstances would point to an early beginning of Greek school life; whereas, on the other hand, the small number of subjects required in those days, the absence from the programme of various languages, of most exact sciences, and of general history and geography, made it unnecessary to begin so early, or work so hard, as our unfortunate children have to do. Above all, there were no competitive examinations, except in athletics and music. The Greeks never thought of promoting a man for 'dead knowledge,' but for his living grasp of science or of life.

Owing to these causes, we find the theorists discussing, as they now do, the expediency of waiting till the age of seven before beginning serious education—some advising it, others recommending easy and half-playing lessons from an earlier period. And then, as now, we find the same curious silence on the really important fact that the exact number of years a child has lived is nothing to the point in question, and that while one child may be too young at seven to commence work, many more may be distinctly too old.

§ 11. At all events, we may assume in parents the same varieties of over-anxiety, of over-indulgence, of nervousness, and of carelessness about their children; and so it doubtless came to pass that there was in many cases a gap between infancy and school-life, which was spent in playing and doing mischief. This may be fairly inferred, not only from such anecdotes as that of Alcibiades playing with his fellows in the street,[1] evidently without the protection of any pædagogue, but also from the large nomen-

[1] Plut. *Alkib.* c. 2.

clature of boys' games preserved to us in the glossaries of later grammarians.

These games are quite distinct from the regular exercises in the palæstra (of which we will speak presently, as forming a regular part of education). We have only general descriptions of them, and these either by Greek scholiasts or by modern philologists. But in spite of the sad want of practical knowledge of games shown by both, the instincts of boyhood are so uniform that we can often frame a very distinct idea of the sort of amusement popular among Greek children. For young boys, games can hardly consist of anything else than either the practising of some bodily dexterity, such as hopping on one foot, higher or longer than is easy, or throwing further with a stone; or else some imitation of war, such as snowballing, or pulling a rope across a line, or pursuing under fixed conditions; or lastly, the practice of some mechanical ingenuity, such as whipping a top, or shooting with marbles. So far as climate or mechanical inventions have not altered our little boys' games, we find all these principles represented in Greek games. There was the *hobby or cock-horse* (κάλαμον παραβῆναι), standing or hopping on one leg (ἀσκωλιάζειν), which, as the word ἀσκός implies, was attempted on a *skin-bottle* filled with liquid and greased; blind-man's buff (χαλκῆ μυῖα), in which the boy cried, 'I am hunting a *brazen fly*,' and the rest answered, 'You will not catch it'; games of hide-and-seek, of taking and releasing prisoners, of fool in the middle, of playing at king—in fact, there is probably no simple child's game now known which was not then in use.

Various Children's Games.

A few more details may, however, be interesting. There was a game called κυνδαλισμός, in which the κύνδαλον was a *peg* of wood with a heavy end sharpened, which boys sought to strike into a softened place in the earth so that it stood upright, and knocked out the peg of a rival. This reminds us of the peg-top splitting which still goes on in our streets. Another, called ὀστρακίνδα, consisted of tossing an *oyster shell* in the air, of which one side was blackened or moistened, and called *night*, the other *day*, or sun and rain. The boys were divided into two sides with these names, and according as their side of the shell turned up, they pursued and took prisoners their adversaries. On the other hand, ἐποστρακισμός was making a *shell* skip along the surface of water by a horizontal throw, and winning by the greatest number of skips. Εἰς ὥμιλλαν, though a general expression for any contest, was specially applied to tossing a knuckle bone or smooth stone so as to lie in the centre of a fixed *circle*, and to disturb those which were already in good positions. This was also done into a small hole (τρόπα). They seem to have shot dried *beans* from their fingers as we do marbles (φρυγίνδα). They spun *coins* on their edge (χαλκισμός).

Here are two games not perhaps so universal now-a-days. Πενταλιθίζειν was a technical word for tossing up *five pebbles* or astragali, and receiving them so as to make them lie on the back of the hand. Μηλολόνθη, or the *beetle* game, consisted in flying a beetle by a long thread, and guiding him like a kite. But by way of improvement they attached a waxed splinter, lighted, to his tail, and this cruelty is now practised, according to a good authority (Papasliotis), in Greece, and has even been known to cause serious fires.[1] Tops were known under various names (βέμβιξ, στρόμβος, στρόβιλος), one of them certainly a humming-top. So were hoops (τροχοί).

Ball playing was ancient and diffused, even among the Homeric heroes. But as it was found very fashionable and carefully practised by both Mexicans and Peruvians at the time of the conquest, it is probably common to all civilised races. We have no details left us of complicated games with balls, and the mere throwing them up and catching them one from the other, with some rythmic motion, is hardly worth all the poetic fervour shown about this game by the Greeks. But possibly the musical and dancing accompaniments were very important, in the case of grown people, and in historical times. Pollux, however—our main authority for most of these games—in one place[2] distinctly describes both football and handball. 'The names,' he says, 'of games with balls are—ἐπίσκυρος, φαινίνδα, ἀπόρραξις, οὐρανία. The first is played by two even sides, who draw a line in the centre, which they called σκῦρος, on which they place the ball. They draw two other lines behind each side, and those who first reach the ball throw it (ῥίπτουσιν) over the opponents, whose duty it is to catch it and return it, until one side drives the other back over their goal line.' Though Pollux makes no mention of *kicking*, this game

---

[1] This seems to be the interpretation of *Achar.* 920 sq. according to Grasberger.
[2] ix. 103.

is evidently our football in substance. He proceeds: 'φαινίνδα was called either from Phænindes, the first discoverer, or from deceiving (φενακίζειν),' &c.—we need not follow his etymologies—' and ἀπόρραξις consists of making a *ball bound* off the ground, and sending it against a wall, counting the number of the hops according as it was returned.' And as if to make the anticipations of our games more curiously complete, there is cited from the history of Manuel, by the Byzantine Cinnamus (A.D. 1200) a clear description of the Canadian La crosse, a sort of hockey played with racquets :—' Certain youths, divided equally, leave in a level place, which they have before prepared and measured, a ball made of leather, about the size of an apple, and rush at it, as if it were a prize lying in the middle, from their fixed starting-point (a goal). Each of them has in his right hand a *racquet* (ῥάβδον) of suitable length ending in a sort of flat bend, the middle of which is occupied by gut strings dried by seasoning, and plaited together in net fashion. Each side strives to be the first to bring it to the opposite end of the ground from that allotted to them. Whenever the ball is driven by the ῥάβδοι (racquet) to the end of the ground it counts as a victory.'[1]

Two games, which were not confined to children, and which are not widely diffused, though they exist, among us, are the use of *astragali*, or knuckle bones of animals,

---

[1] I do not know whether so late an authority is valid proof for the early Greek origin of a game. Most certainly the polo played at Constantinople at the same time came from an equestrian people, and not from the Greeks.

so cut nearly square as to serve for dice, and with these children threw for luck, the highest throw (sixes) being accounted the best. In later Greek art representations of Eros and other youthful figures engaged with astragali are frequent. It is to be feared that this game was an introduction to dice-playing, which was so common, and so often abused, that among the few specimens of ancient dice remaining, there are some false and which were evidently loaded. The other game to which I allude is the Italian *morra*, the guessing instantaneously how many fingers are thrown up by the player and his adversary. It is surprising how fond southern men and boys still are of this simple game, chiefly, however, for gambling purposes.

There was tossing in a blanket, walking on stilts, swinging, leap-frog, and many other similar plays, which are ill-understood, and worse explained, by the learned, and of no importance to us, save as proving the general similarity of the life of little boys then as now.

We know nothing about the condition of little girls of the same age, except that they specially indulged in ball-playing. Like our own children, the girls probably joined, to a lesser degree, in the boys' games, and only so far as they could be carried on within doors, in the court of the house. There are graceful representations of their swinging and practising our *see-saw*. Dolls they had in plenty, and doll-making (of clay) was quite a special trade at Athens. In more than one instance we have found in children's graves their favourite dolls, which sorrowing parents laid with them as a sort of keepsake in the tomb.

§ 12. Most unfortunately there is hardly a word left of

the nursery rimes, and of the folk lore, which are very much more interesting than the physical amusements of children. Yet we know that such popular songs existed in plenty; we know, too, from the early fame of Æsop's fables, from the myths so readily invented and exquisitely told by Plato, that here we have lost a real fund of beautiful and stimulating children's stories.[1] And of course here, too, the general character of such stories throughout the human race was preserved.

[1] There is a possibility of recovering some of them by a careful collection of the ναναρίσματα of the modern Greeks, which in many cases doubtless correspond to their forerunners the βαυκαλήματα of the old Greeks. Stories of *Mormo* and *Gorgo* and the *Empousa* are still current to frighten children, as are also (about Arachova) songs about Charos (the old Charon), the ruthless genius of death. The belief in Lamia is still so common, that ἔπνιξεν ἡ Λάμια—*Lamia choked it*—is a common expression when a child dies suddenly. Cf. Βενιζέλος, *On the Private Life of the Old Greeks* (Athens, 1873).

CHAPTER III.

SCHOOL DAYS—THE PHYSICAL SIDE.

§ 13. THE most striking difference between early Greek education and ours was undoubtedly this: that the physical development of boys was attended to in a special place and by a special master. It was not thought sufficient for them to play the chance games of childhood; they underwent careful bodily training under a very fixed system, which was determined by the athletic contests of after life. This feature, which excites the admiration of the modern Germans, and has given rise to an immense literature, is doubtless all the more essential now that the mental training of our boys has become so much more trying; and we can quite feel, when we look at the physical development of ordinary foreigners, how keenly they must envy the freedom of limb and ease of motion, not only as we see it suggested by Greek statues, but as we have it before us in the ordinary sporting Englishman. But it is quite in accordance with their want of practical development, that while they write immense books about the physical training of the Greeks, and the possibility of imitating it in modern education, they seem quite ignorant of that side of English education at our public schools; and yet there they might see in practice a physical education in no way inferior to that described in classical authors. I say it quite deliberately—the public school boy, who is trained in cricket, football, and rowing, and who in his holidays can obtain riding, salmon fishing, hunting, and shooting, enjoys a physical training which no classical days ever equalled. The athletic part of this training is enjoyed by all boys at our public schools, though the field sports at home only fall to the lot of the richer or more fortunate.

§ 14. When we compare what the Greeks afforded to their boys, we find it divided into two contrasted kinds of exercise: hunting, which was practised by the Spartans very keenly, and no doubt also by the Eleans and Arcadians, as may be seen from Xenophon's *Tract on [Hare] Hunting;* and gymnastics, which in the case of boys were carried on in the so-called *palæstra*, a sort of open air gymnasium (in our sense) kept by private individuals as a speculation, and to which the boys were sent, as they were to their ordinary schoolmaster.[1] We find that the Spartans, who had ample scope for hunting with dogs in the glens and coverts of Mount Taygetus,

---

[1] The exact relation of the ancient *palæstra* and the *gymnasium* has much exercised the critics. It seems plain that the former was a private establishment, and intended for boys; the latter more general, and resorted to by young men, not only amateurs and beginners, but also more accomplished athletes. Hence the terms are often confused. In the *Tract on the Athenian State*, however, the author mentions *palæstras* as built by the demos for its public use, and this tract, whoever may be its author, does not date later than 415 B.C.

rather despised mere exercises of dexterity in the palæstra, just as our sportsmen would think very little of spending hours in a gymnasium. But those Greeks who lived in towns like Athens, and in the midst of a thickly populated and well-cultivated country, could not possibly obtain hunting, and therefore found the most efficient substitute.

Still we find them very far behind the English in their knowledge or taste for out-of-door games, such as cricket, football, hockey, golf, &c.—games which combine chance and skill, which combine strength with dexterity, and which intensely interest the players while keeping them in the open air Yachting, though there were regattas, was not in fashion in ancient Greece. Rowing, which they could have practised to their heart's content, and which was of the last importance in their naval warfare, was never thought gentlemanly, and always consigned to slaves or hirelings. There are indeed, as above quoted from Pollux, descriptions of some thing like football and La crosse, but the obscurity and rarity of any allusions to them show that they are in no sense national games. Running races round a short course was one of their chief exercises, but this is no proper out-of-door game.

§ 15. Accordingly, the Germans, in seeking to base their physical education on Greek lines, seem to make the capital mistake of ignoring that kind of exercise for boys, which vastly exceeds in value any training in gymnasia. The Eton and Harrow match at Lord's is a far more beautiful sight, and far better for the performers, than the boys' wrestling or running at Olympia. And besides the variety of exercise at a game like cricket, and the various intelligence and decision which it stimulates, a great part of the game lies not in the winning, but in the proper *form* of the play, in what the Greeks so highly prized as *eurythmy*, a graceful action not merely in dancing and ball-playing, but in the most violent physical exertion.

But the Greeks had no playgrounds beyond the palæstra or gymnasium; they had no playgrounds in our sense, and though a few proverbs speak of swimming as a universal accomplishment which boys learned, the silence of Greek literature on the subject[1] makes one very suspicious as to the generality of such training.

With this introduction, we may turn to some details as to the education of Greek boys in their *palæstra*.

§ 16. In one point, certainly, the Greeks agreed more with the modern English than with any other civilised nation. They regarded sport as a really serious thing. And unless it is so regarded, it will never be brought to the national perfection to which the English have brought it, or to which the Greeks are supposed to have brought it. And yet even in this point the Greeks regarded their sports differently from us, and from all nations who have adopted Semitic ideas in religion. Seriousness of the religious kind is with us quite distinct from the seriousness of sport. With the Greeks it was not, or rather seriousness was not with them an attribute of religion in any sense more than it was of ordinary life. They har-

---

[1] Herodotus, indeed (viii. 89), speaks of the generality of Greek sailors as able to swim.

monised religion and sports not by the seriousness of their sports so much as by the cheerfulness—a Semite, ancient or modern, would say by the levity—of their deities; *for the gods, too, love sport* (φιλοπαίγμονες γὰρ καὶ οἱ θεοί), says Plato in his *Cratylus*, a remarkable and thoroughly Greek utterance. The greatest feasts of the gods were celebrated by intensifying human pleasures— not merely those of the palate, according to the grosser notion of the Christian middle ages, but æsthetical pleasures, and that of excitement, pleasures, not of idleness, but of keen enjoyment.

§ 17. The names applied to the exercising-places indicate their principal uses. *Palæstra* means a wrestling-place; *gymnasium* originally a place for naked exercise, but the word early lost this connotation and came to mean mere physical training. We hear that a short *race-course* (δρόμος) was often attached to the palæstra, and short it must have been, for it was sometimes covered in (called ξυστός), probably with a shed roof along the wall of the main inclosure.

There is no evidence to decide the point whether the boys went to this establishment at the same age that they went to school, and at a different hour of the day, or at a different age, taking their physical and mental education separately. And even in this latter case we are left in doubt which side obtained the priority. The best authorities among the Germans decide on separate ages for palæstra and school, and put the palæstra first. But in the face of many uncertainties, and some evidence the other way, the common sense view is preferable that both kinds of instruction were given together, though we know nothing about the distribution of the day, save that both are asserted to have begun very early. Even the theoretical schemes of Plato and Aristotle do not help us here, and it is one of those many points which are now lost on account of their being once so perfectly obvious and familiar.

We here discuss the physical side first, because it is naturally consequent upon the home games, which have been described, and because the mental side will naturally connect itself with the higher education of more advanced years. And here, too, of the great divisions of exercises in the palæstra—*wrestling* and *dancing*, more properly exercises of strength and of grace—we will place athletics first, as the other naturally leads us on to the mental side.

§ 18. In order to leave home and reach the palæstra safely as well as to return, Greek boys were put under the charge of a *pædagogue*, in no way to be identified (as it now is) with a schoolmaster. The text, 'The law was our schoolmaster, to bring us unto Christ,' has suffered from this mistake. The Greek *pædagogue* means merely the slave who had the charge of bringing his master's sons safely to and from school, and guarding them from mischief by the way. He was often old and trusty, often old and useless, always ignorant, and never respected. He was evidently regarded by young and gay boys as a great interference to enjoyment, insisting upon punctual hours of return, and limiting that intercourse with elder boys which was so fascinating, but also so dangerous to Greek children.

The keeper of the palæstra and *trainer* (παιδοτρίβης) was not appointed by the State, but (as already mentioned) took up the work as a private enterprise, not directed by, but under the supervision of, the State, in the way of police regulation. We have, indeed, in the speech of Æschines *against Timarchus*, very stringent laws quoted to the effect that no palæstra or school might be open before or after daylight; that no one above boys' age might enter or remain in the building, and the severest penalties, even death, were imposed on the violation of these regulations. But we know that, even if true, which is very doubtful, the text of the laws here cited became a dead letter, for it was a favourite resort of elder men to see the boys exercising. Restrictions there were, of course; a fashionable lounge could in no way serve as a strict training school, and we know that at Sparta, even in the gymnasia, the regulation *strip or go* was enforced to prevent an idle crowd.

§ 19. There is figured on many vases, often in brilliant colours, the interior of the palæstra. It is denoted by the bearded Hermes—a rude bust of the patron god. A middle-aged man in a short mantle or *chlamys*, with a rod or wand in his hand, is watching and directing the exercises of the boys, generally a wrestling match. We know also from the *pentathlon* being once introduced at Olympia for boys, that its five exercises were those in which they were usually trained—leaping, running, throwing the discus, the spear, and wrestling. For elder boys, boxing and the *pancratium* were doubtless added, if they meant to train for public competitions, but ordinary gentlemen's sons would never undergo this special training and its hardships. Indeed, the Spartans strictly discountenanced such sports, both as likely to disfigure, and as sure to produce quarrels and ill will. The lighter exercises were intended to make the frame hardy, and the movements graceful, and were introduced by a thorough rubbing of the skin with olive oil, which, after the training, was scraped off with a special instrument, the στλεγγίς, as may be seen in the splendid Vatican statue of the athlete scraping his arm, the so-called *Apoxyomenos*, referred to as an original of Lysippus. In luxurious days they also took a bath, but this was hardly the case with ordinary boys—indeed, the water supply of Greek towns was probably scanty enough, and the nation not given to much washing.

§ 20. There remain little or no details as to the exact rules of training practised in the ordinary palæstras, but we may fairly assume them to have been the same in kind (though milder in degree) as those approved for formal athletes. If we judge from these, we will not form a high idea of Greek training. Pausanias informs us that they trained on dry cheese, which is not surprising, as they were (like most southerns) not a very carnivorous people. But when a known athlete (Dromeus [1]) discovered that meat diet was the best, they seem to have followed up the discovery by inferring that the more of a good thing the better, and so athletes were required to eat very large quantities of meat, owing to which they were lazy and sleepy when not engaged in active work.[2] We need not

[1] Paus. vi. 7, 9.
[2] It was a curious rule at the Olympic games that the com-

suppose that the diet of ordinary boys was in any way interfered with, but this particular case shows the crude notions which prevailed, and the trainer came more and more to assume the part of a dietetic doctor, as is stated by Plato.

§ 21. So much as to the conditions of good training; as to the performance, there are points of no less significance. All the learned Germans who write on these subjects notice that the Olympic races were carried out on soft sand, not on hard and springy ground, so that really good pace cannot have been a real object to Greek runners.[1] But what is worse, they praise their zeal and energy in starting (as we see on vases) with wild swinging of their arms, in spread-eagle fashion, and *encouraging themselves with loud shouts*.[2] This style of running may seem very fine to a professor in his study, but will only excite ridicule among those who have ever made the least practical essay, or seen any competitions. But possibly the Greeks were not so uniformly silly in this respect as they are now represented by commentators, for there is preserved on the Acropolis at Athens one

---

petitors were even compelled to swear that they had spent a month in training at Elis, as if it mattered whether the victory was won by natural endowments only, or by careful study. One would have thought that the importance of the contest would ensure ample training among those who desired to win.

[1] I myself saw at the Olympic games now held at Athens in the re-excavated *stadion* of Herodes, a sprint-race of 200 yards over vine ground, cut into furrows, with dogs and people obstructing the course. Cf. *Macmillan's Magazine* for September 1876.

[2] Cf. for example, Grasberger, *Erziehung, &c.*, iii. 212, quoting Cicero, *Tusc. Disp.* ii. 23, 56.

Greek Beauty exaggerated. 33

little known vase, on which a running figure has the elbows held tightly back in the proper way. We may also have grave suspicions about Greek boxing, from the facts that they weighted the hand heavily with loaded gloves, and that boxers are described as men with their *ears*, and not with their *noses*, crushed. We cannot but suspect them of swinging round and not striking straight from the shoulder. This is further proved by the use of protecting *ear-caps* (ἀμφωτίδες) in boxing, a thing which no modern boxer would dream of doing.

§ 22. All these hints taken together make us reasonably suspect that, *as athletics*, the training of the *Pædotribes* was not what we should admire. But, on the other hand, the picturesque and enthusiastic descriptions of beautiful and well-trained Greek boys, coupled with the ideal figures which remain to us in Greek sculpture, prove beyond any doubt that they knew perfectly what a beautiful manly form was, and by what training it could be produced. Let us, however, not exaggerate the matter. Very few boys really equalled the ideal types of the sculptor, and if we make allowance for this, we may conclude that the finest English public-school boy is not inferior to the best Greek types in real life.[1] Perhaps some advantage may have resulted from the greater freedom of limb

---

[1] It is a perpetual and perhaps now ineradicable mistake, because we cannot see the real Athenians or Spartans of classical days, to imagine them *in general* like the ideal statues of the Greek artists. We find it even generally stated that beauty was the rule, and ugliness the exception, among them, in spite of Cicero's complaint, when he was disillusioned by a visit to Athens : ' Quotusquisque enim formosus est ? Quum Athenis essem e gregibus epheborum vix singuli reperiebantur.'

obtained by naked training, and rubbing with oil; but the advantage of this over a modern flannel suit, or tight athlete's dress, is very small. Nevertheless, the English schoolboy is physically so superior to the schoolboys of other European nations that we may count him, with the Greek boy, as almost a distinct animal.

What surprises us is that by regular training in the simplest exercises, such as running, leaping, wrestling, and throwing the discus or dart, such splendid results were ever attained. Or shall we say, that it was not the *wrestling*, but the *dancing* side of Greek training which was of chief importance? We may dismiss with a word the fabulous stories of athletic feats at Olympia, where a certain Chionis, a Spartan of early date (Ol. 28-31, *circ.* 660 B.C.), was said to have leapt 52 feet, and afterwards Phayllus of Croton 55 feet. We may infer, too, from the use of *weights* (ἁλτῆρες) that the jump was a standing one. Happily these assertions are only made by late grammarians, and though some German critics are inclined to extend their adoration of Greek training to this point, it will rather, with practical readers, tend to discredit other statements made by the same authority. As we do not hear of a running jump, so we do not hear of a high jump either, at least in public games. Both may have been practised in the palæstra. The distance for a sprint-race for men was 200 yards, and somewhat shorter for boys. Their longest race at Olympia was 24 stadia (4,800 yards, $2\frac{2}{3}$ miles), which the professors, without any knowledge of the time in which it was done, think more wonderful than the 55 feet jump, but which is equalled in many English sports of the present day.

§ 23. Apart from the doubts here raised as to the perfection of Greek training, let us revert, in conclusion, to the absence among elder boys of those out-of-door games like cricket, which are so valuable for developing mental together with physical qualities. There is one feature in these games which the Greeks seem to have missed altogether, and which appears to be ignored in most German books on the reform of physical education in schools. It is that forming of clubs and teams of boys, in which they choose their own leaders, and get accustomed to self-government, and a submission to the superior will of equals, or the decision of public opinion among themselves. Plato saw long ago that the proper and peculiar intention of boys' sports was more mental than bodily improvement. But he confined himself to that part of the question which advocates the cultivation of spirit in boys, as better than that which cultivates strength only. This is perfectly true, and no game is worthy the name in which spirit and intelligence cannot defeat brute strength. But there is little trace, save at Sparta, of any free constitution in boys' education, in which they manage their own affairs, fight out their own quarrels, and praise or censure according to a public opinion of their own. No Greek educator seems to have had an inkling of this, and the foreign theorists who have discussed educational reforms on the Greek models seem equally unaware of its importance. Yet here, if anywhere, is the secret of that independence of character and self-reliance which is the backbone of the English constitution and the national liberty. The Greeks were like the French and the Germans, who always imagine that the games and sports will not prosper or be properly conducted without the supervision of a Turnlehrer or overseer, and they give great exhortations to this man to sympathise with the boys and stimulate them. In England the main duty of such people is to keep out of the way, and let the boys manage their own affairs. The results of the opposed systems will strike anyone who compares, on the one hand, the neat and well-regulated French boys of a boarding school, walking two and two with gloves on and toes turned out, along a road, followed by a master; on the other, the playgrounds of any good English school during recreation time. If the zealous and learned reformers, who write books on the subject in modern Europe, would take the trouble to come and see this for themselves, it might modify both their encomia on Greek training and their suggestions for their own countries.

CHAPTER IV.

SCHOOL DAYS—THE MUSICAL SIDE—THE SCHOOLMASTER.

§ 24. WE will approach this side of the question by quoting the famous description of Greek education in Plato's *Protagoras*,[1] which will recall to the reader the general problem, so apt to be lost or obscured amid details. 'Education and admonition commence in the very first years of childhood, and last to the very end of life. Mother and nurse and father and *tutor* (παιδαγωγός) are quarrelling about the improvement of the child as soon as ever he is able to understand them; he cannot say or do anything without their setting forth to him that this is just and that is unjust; that this is honourable, that is dishonourable; this is holy, that is unholy; do this, and abstain from that. And if he obeys, well and good; if not, he is straightened by threats and blows, like a piece of warped wood. At a later stage, they send him to teachers, and enjoin them to see to his manners even more than to his reading and music; and the teachers do as they are desired. And when the boy has

[1] p. 325 c. Cf. also Axiochus, p. 366, E : ὁπόταν δὲ εἰς τὴν ἐπταετίαν ἀφίκηται [τὸ νήπιον] πολλοὺς πόνους διαντλῆσαν, παιδαγωγοί καὶ γραμματισταί καὶ παιδοτρίβαι τυραννοῦντες, κ.τ.λ.

learned his letters, and is beginning to understand what is written, as before he understood only what was spoken, they put into his hands the works of great poets, which he reads at school; in these are contained many admonitions, and many tales and praises, and encomia of ancient famous men, which he is required to learn by heart, in order that he may imitate or emulate them, and desire to become like them. Then, again, the teachers of the lyre take similar care that their young disciple is steady and gets into no mischief; and when they have taught him the use of the lyre, they introduce him to the works of other excellent poets, who are the lyric poets; and these they set to music, and make their harmonies and rythms quite familiar to the children, in order that they may learn to be more gentle, and harmonious, and rythmical, and so more fitted for speech and action; for the life of man in every part has need of harmony and rythm. Then they send them to the master of gymnastic, in order that their bodies may better minister to the virtuous mind, and that the weakness of their bodies may not force them to play the coward in war or on any other occasion. This is what is done by those who have the means, and those who have the means are the rich; their children begin education soonest and leave off latest. When they have done with masters, the State again compels them to learn the laws, and live after the pattern which they furnish, and not after their own fancies; and just as in learning to write, the writing master first draws lines with a stylus for the use of the young beginner, and gives him the tablet, and makes him follow the lines, so the city draws the laws, which were

Traditional Education. 39

the invention of good lawgivers which were of old time; these are given to the young man in order to guide him in his conduct whether as ruler or ruled; and he who transgresses them is to be corrected or called to account, which is a term used not only in your country, but in many others.'

This is the argument put by Plato into the mouth of Protagoras the sophist, to show that virtue is a thing which can be taught, and not a mere natural predisposition or a divine grace. The other *locus classicus*, which may be referred to in close connection with it, is the description of the traditional education given in Aristophanes' *Clouds*.[1] The strict discipline of boys who were

[1] 961 sq. :

λέξω τοίνυν τὴν ἀρχαίαν παιδείαν, ὡς διέκειτο,
ὅτ' ἐγὼ τὰ δίκαια λέγων ἤνθουν καὶ σωφροσύνη νενόμιστο.
πρῶτον μὲν ἔδει παιδὸς φωνὴν γρύξαντος μηδέν' ἀκοῦσαι·
εἶτα βαδίζειν ἐν ταῖσιν ὁδοῖς εὐτάκτως εἰς κιθαριστοῦ
τοὺς κωμήτας γυμνοὺς ἀθρόους, κεἰ κριμνώδη κατανίφοι.
εἶτ' αὖ προμαθεῖν ᾆσμ' ἐδίδασκεν, τὼ μηρὼ μὴ ξυνέχοντας,
ἢ Παλλάδα περσέπολιν δεινὰν, ἢ Τηλέπορόν τι βόαμα,
ἐντειναμένους τὴν ἁρμονίαν, ἣν οἱ πατέρες παρέδωκαν.
εἰ δέ τις αὐτῶν βωμολοχεύσαιτ' ἢ κάμψειέν τινα καμπὴν,
οἵας οἱ νῦν τὰς κατὰ Φρῦνιν ταύτας τὰς δυσκολοκάμπτους,
ἀπετρίβετο τυπτόμενος πολλὰς ὡς τὰς Μούσας ἀφανίζων.
ἐν παιδοτρίβου δὲ καθίζοντας τὸν μηρὸν ἔδει προβαλέσθαι
τοὺς παῖδας, ὅπως τοῖς ἔξωθεν μηδὲν δείξειαν ἀπηνές·
εἶτ' αὖ πάλιν αὖθις ἀνιστάμενον συμψῆσαι, καὶ προνοεῖσθαι
εἴδωλον τοῖσιν ἐρασταῖσιν τῆς ἥβης μὴ καταλείπειν.
ἠλείψατο δ' ἂν τοὐμφαλοῦ οὐδεὶς παῖς ὑπένερθεν τότ' ἄν, ὥστε
τοῖς αἰδοίοισι δρόσος καὶ χνοῦς ὥσπερ μήλοισιν ἐπήνθει·
οὐδ' ἂν μαλακὴν φυρασάμενος τὴν φωνὴν πρὸς τὸν ἐραστὴν
αὐτὸς ἑαυτὸν προαγωγεύων τοῖς ὀφθαλμοῖς ἐβάδιζεν,
οὐδ' ἂν ἑλέσθαι δειπνοῦντ' ἐξῆν κεφάλαιον τῆς ῥαφανῖδος,
οὐδ' ἄννηθον τῶν πρεσβυτέρων ἁρπάζειν οὐδὲ σέλινον,
οὐδ' ὀψοφαγεῖν, οὐδὲ κιχλίζειν, οὐδ' ἴσχειν τὼ πόδ' ἐναλλάξ, κ.τ.λ.

not allowed to utter a whisper before their elders, who were sent in troops early in the morning to school, in their single tunic, even in the deepest winter snow, who were kept at work with the music master studying old traditional hymns, and in attitudes strictly controlled as regards modesty and decency—all this is contrasted by the poet with what he considers the corruption of the youth with florid and immoral music, their meretricious desire to exhibit their bodily and mental perfections, their luxury and sloth, their abandonment of sobriety and diligence.

There are peculiarities of Greek taste so openly alluded to in this passage that it will not bear literal translation into English, at least into a book for ordinary readers, and therefore it need only be remarked in criticism of it that too much stress has been laid by theorists on Greek life, both on the picture of over-anxious morality in the older time, and on the alleged immorality of the poet's age. It is from such passages that German historians draw their very extravagant assertions of the rapid degeneracy of the Athenians under what they call the *ochlocracy*, which followed upon the death of Pericles. It is very easy to find in many other ages and times similar assertions of the glory of the good old times, and the degeneracy of the satirist's own contemporaries. But there is generally no more truth in it than in the assertion of Homer, that his heroes took up and threw easily great rocks which two, or five, or ten men, such as they now are, could not lift. The same sort of thing was said in poetry of the mediæval knights, in comparison with modern Europe. One would imagine them of greater size and might than we are, and yet their suits of armour are seldom large enough for a man of six feet high. The picture of Aristophanes is doubtless a deliberate exaggeration, and would have been readily acknowledged as such by the poet himself. But it of course gives us the extremes possible in real life, as he knew it, and is therefore of use in forming our ideas on the question, if we use common sense and caution.

§ 25. With the exception of this feature, that Greek parents showed a greater apprehension for the morals of their boys, and guarded them as we should guard the morals of girls, it will be seen that the principles of education are permanent, and applicable in all ages under similar circumstances.

But what the ancients called *music* in the wider sense must be held to include a knowledge and recitation of good poetry, as well as proper training in that figured dancing which was the most usual service of the gods. Indeed, a good musical education in Greece, much in contrast to ours, included every graceful æsthetical and intellectual accomplishment. This wide use of the term, however, though co-ordinate with the ordinary sense of playing instruments and singing, causes little confusion. A distinction between 'music and singing,' such as we often see it (not satirically) set forth in the advertisements of our professional teachers, was not admitted.

§ 26. I think we may be justified in asserting that the study of the epic poets, especially of the Iliad and Odyssey, was the earliest intellectual exercise of schoolboys, and, in the case of fairly educated parents, even anticipated the learning of letters. For the latter is never spoken of as part of a mother's or of home education. Reading was not so universal or so necessary as it now is, and as it was in earlier days an accomplishment only gradually becoming an essential, its acquisition seems always to have been entrusted to a professional master, the γραμματιστής, or *grammarian* in the earlier use of the word. Of course careful parents, of the model above set forth by Protagoras, must have inculcated early lessons from poetry before that age. We may assume that books of Homer were read or recited to growing boys, and that they were encouraged or required to learn them off by heart.

This is quite certain to all who estimate justly the enormous influence ascribed to Homer, and the principles assumed by the Greeks to have underlain his work. He was universally considered to be a *moral teacher*, whose characters were drawn with a moral intent, and for the purpose of example or avoidance. In Plato's *Ion* we distinctly find something supernatural, some distinct inspiration by the muse, asserted of Homer, and this inspiration was even passed on, like some magnetic force, from bard to bard. These ancient poets were even supposed to have uttered words deeper and holier than they themselves knew, being driven by some divine *œstrus* to compose what they could not have said in their natural state. Accordingly the Iliad and Odyssey were supposed to contain all that was useful, not only for godliness, but for life. All the arts and sciences were to be derived (by interpretation) from these sacred texts.

Hence, when it occurs to a modern reader that the main superiority of our education over the Greek is the early training in the Scriptures—a training, alas! decaying in earnestness every day—an old Athenian, or Milesian, or Cean would deny the fact, and say that they, too, had an inspired volume, written for their learning, in which all the moral virtues, and all the necessaries of faith were contained. The charge of objectionable passages in the old Epic would doubtless be retorted by a similar charge against the old Semitic books.

§ 27. It is well-nigh impossible that in the higher families throughout Greece this moral training should not have begun at home; and there must have been many Greek mothers able and anxious to help, though history is silent about them, and does not even single out individual cases, like the Roman Cornelia, where mothers influenced the moral and intellectual training of their children.[1] Certain it is that here and there we find evidences of a strong feeling of respect to the house-mother which contrast curiously with the usual silence about women. In the *Clouds*, the acme of villainy in the young scapegrace, who has turned sophist under Socrates' hands, is to threaten violence to his mother.[2] Here it is that Strepsiades exclaims in real horror at the result of such teaching. We also find both Plato and (perhaps

---

[1] Two or three stories of Spartan mothers in Plutarch form tardy and unimportant exceptions.
[2] v. 1444 sq.

in imitation of him) Cicero laying stress upon the purity of speech preserved in the conversation of cultivated women, whose conservative life and tastes rejected slang and novelty, and thus preserved the language pure and undefiled. The very opposite complaint is made concerning the *pædagogues*, whose often barbarous origin and rude manners were of damage to the youth.

§ 28. On the question of punishments, both at home and at school, we do not find the Greeks very different from ourselves. There are not in Greek literature any such eloquent protests against corporal punishment as we find in Seneca and Quintilian. They all acknowledge the use and justice of it, and only caution against applying servile punishments to free boys. Indeed, in many later writers, such as Lucian, the severities of schoolmasters are noted, and we have among the Pompeian pictures a scene of a master flogging a boy, who is hoisted on the shoulders of another, with a third holding him up by the heels. These evidences, together with those of the later Romans, on the sounds of woe common in schools, must not be overestimated. They are probably exceptional cases made prominent for satirical purposes, and not implying any peculiar savagery in Greek above modern masters.

Most certainly the Greek schoolmaster was not harsher than the lower class masters in many primary schools, as for example, the Irish hedge schoolmasters described in Carleton's *Tales of the Irish Peasantry*.

Unfortunately, the Greek schoolmaster, at least of elementary schools, was not generally in high repute, was evidently not highly paid, and his calling was not such as to give him either dignity or self-respect. He was accused of pedantry if he was really learned, and of bad temper if he was zealous and impatient at idleness.[1]

Lucian, in a jocose description of the nether world, describes kings and satraps as beggars or 'primary' schoolmasters, and was only carrying out into fiction the proverbial downfall of the tyrant Dionysius of Syracuse, who spent his old age teaching children at Corinth. An unknown comic writer is quoted as saying, 'the man is either dead or teaching the alphabet.' We hear of philosophers accusing each other—very absurdly—of having once followed this profession, and every scholar will remember the famous passage in Demosthenes' *De Corona*, 'But you, worthy man, who despise others compared with yourself, now compare with mine your own lot, which consigned you to grow up from boyhood in the greatest need, when you helped your father to attend in the school, preparing the ink, cleaning the benches, sweeping out the schoolroom, and so taking the rank of a slave and not of a free boy.' We even hear of Horace's master Orbilius writing a lamentable autobiography on account of his

---

[1] Cf. the amusing notes in Cicero's letters on a private tutor he got for his son and nephew, vi. 1, 9: 'I am in love with Dionysius. The boys say he flies into furious passions. But no man could be more learned or conscientious (*sanctior*) or more devoted to you and me.' Presently Cicero's tone alters, viii. 4: 'Dionysius gave me impudence—you would say I had procured another Dicæarchus or Aristoxenus, and not a man that talks us all down, and is no good for teaching. But he has a good memory.'

miseries, under the title of *the man acquainted with grief* (περιαλγής).

§ 29. The general question of the payment of teachers will be better discussed when we come to the Sophists' training of riper youth. Indeed, on the whole value of the various attacks on the teaching order in Greece, Grasberger concludes his elaborate summary of the above, and many other, facts with the sensible remark :[1] 'As regards the unpleasant and objectionable features, which men seem to record with special preference, the true state of the case may be the same as with the many scandals which are reported from the life of the mediæval universities in Europe. Evil did not predominate ; but the chronicler, instead of putting forward the modest virtues of diligence and of scientific earnestness, preferred to note both the faults of the teachers and the gross excesses of the students.'

We may be sure that in the Greek primary schools, though we hear of one assistant sometimes, the master was required to teach all the subjects. This was so not long ago in England, and still more in Ireland, where the hedge schoolmasters, but lately supplanted by the national school system (not without considerable loss), were required, and were able, to teach classics, mathematics, and the old-fashioned English. It is indeed clearly presupposed in all the many bequests of pious benefactors, who leave 40*l*. or 60*l*. per annum for the payment of a single master to keep a school in some remote part of the country. And at Athens, as in the days of these

[1] ii. p. 189.

One Master for all Subjects. 47

bequests, there was no official or state test of a master's qualifications. Each man set up on his private account; it depended on the reputation he made whether his school was well attended. The worthy pedant in Goldsmith's *Deserted Village* gives us a fair specimen of the better class of such men.

CHAPTER V.

THE MUSICAL SIDE—SCHOOLS AND THEIR APPOINTMENTS.

§ 30. THE school was generally distinguished by the term διδασκαλεῖον[1] from the palæstra. We know that every Greek town possessed one or more, and in early times Herodotus[2] mentions one existing at Chios as early as 500 B.C., of which the roof fell in and killed 119 out of 120 children at work within it at the time. Pausanias tells of another at Astypalæa, into which a madman rushed and pulled down the supporting pillar, so that 60 boys were buried under the ruins. The sad affair of Mycalessus is told by Thucydides, and extorts from him a most ungrammatical grimace of pity, when Thracian mercenaries murdered all the children assembled in school. These cases show how it was evidently regarded as an essential in every town. So the Trœzenians, when they received the fugitive Athenians during the invasion of Xerxes, took care, even in that great and sudden crisis, to provide for the teaching of the Attic children.[3]

---

[1] διδασκάλιον is the thing learnt.   [2] vi. 27.
[3] The Greek form of our word school, though in common use, meant *leisure*, and only passed through its application to the

School Arrangements.

Of course, in early days, and in poor towns, the place of teaching was not well appointed, nay, even in many places, teaching in the open air prevailed. The oldest legends speak of Cheiron teaching in his grotto on Pelion; in the latest Greek χαμαιδιδάσκαλος (*teacher on the ground*) is a word for a low class of teacher. This was again like the old hedge schools of Ireland, and no doubt of Scotland too. They also took advantage, especially in hot weather, of colonnades, or shady corners among public buildings, as at Winchester the summer term was called *cloister-time,* from a similar practice, even in that wealthy foundation, of instructing in the cloisters.

On the other hand, properly appointed schools in respectable towns were furnished with some taste, and according to traditional notions. As in gymnasia and palæstras, there was a shrine of the Muses or of Hermes, and the head of the institution was regarded as the priest of this shrine, at which offerings were made, so in the schools also there were statues of tutelary gods set up, and busts of heroes, and other eminent men, by way of ornament, as well as reminder to the boys.

We hear that the master sat on a high seat, from which he taught; the scholars often sat on the ground, as they still do in many countries, or else they stood, or occupied benches round him. The pictures and descrip-

leisurely discussions of philosophers into its new and opposite sense. There is some difficulty about the word παιδαγωγεῖον, which some have imagined to be a waiting-room for the pædagogue slaves—absurdly enough. It is probably a mere synonym for the schoolroom

tions extant do not point to the schools being so crowded, as appears from the accidents above cited; but this is probably a mere chance, or an omission for the artist's convenience. For though the laws quoted in Æschines' speech forbid any one save the master and boys to be present, we know that in later days this was not strictly observed, and in Theophrastus' *Characters*, the Chatterbox, among other mistakes in tact, is represented going into the schools and interrupting lessons with his idle talk. We may be sure that there were no tables or desks, such furniture being unusual in Greek houses; it was the universal custom, while reading or writing, to hold the book or roll on the knee—to us an inconvenient thing to do, but still common in the East.

There are some interesting sentences, given for exercise in Greek and Latin, in the little known *Interpretamenta* of Dositheus, now edited and explained by German scholars. The entry of the boy is thus described, in parallel Greek and Latin: 'First I salute the master, who returns my salute: Good morning, master; good morning, schoolfellows. Give me my place, my seat, my stool. Sit closer. Move up that way. This is my place, I took it first.' This mixture of politeness and wrangling is amusing, and no doubt to be found in all ages. It seems that the seats were movable. A scholium on Æschines tells us that there was a supply of water close at hand, lest the boys might suffer from thirst.

The extant pictures show that along the walls were hung up various vessels of which the use is not always plain to us. But we can clearly distinguish the necessary implements for the teaching of reading and writing, boxes for book-rolls, writing-boards, reckoning boards with parallel grooves, and pebbles fixed in them, geometrical figures, flute cases, and lyres. There is also late authority to show that there were notice boards on which regulations were posted. We hear from Lucian of a notice over a sophist's door, 'No philosophy to-day.' The notice board was called 'the white board,' being covered with chalk. We are not told how this was written on, but if the ground was black, then mere writing with the finger across the chalked surface would produce distinct characters.

§ 31. What is far more interesting is the remnant now discovered of the pictorial teaching of children, by hanging up in the schoolroom illustrations of the Trojan and other legends. By the researches of Böttiger and O. Jahn,[1] it appears that we still have the fragments of such a table in the *tabula Iliaca* of Theodorus, preserved at the Capitoline Museum in Rome. These were large pictures, in a series, with names or words of explanation attached to them. Thus we have one picture (from Iliad A) of Chryses praying Agamemnon to restore his daughter, beside him a waggon loaded with ransom, and under each figure, and under the waggon respectively, *Agamemnon, Chryses, the ransom*. Other extant pictures illustrate the third and twenty-fourth books of the Iliad. The Odyssey was similarly treated, so that there seems to have been a traditional and widely circulated pictorial compendium of the Homeric poems used at all events

---

[1] Grasberger, ii. 224.

in later Greek and in Roman schools. There are also chronological and historical fragments of the same kind still extant, so that it is more than probable, that even in classical days Greek boys were not without the benefit of illustrated school books, or at least school sheets, as the elegiac distich on the back of one of them suggests.[1] The use of these pictures on the walls explains the constant appearance of a long wand in the master's hand, which is more characteristic of him than the rod of punishment, though this, too, was not missing.

THE SUBJECTS AND METHOD OF EDUCATION— THE THREE R'S.

§ 32. The usual subdivision of education was into three parts; *letters* (γράμματα), including reading, writing, counting, and learning of the poets; *music* in the stricter sense, including singing and playing on the lyre; and lastly *gymnastic*, which included dancing. These were under the special direction of three classes of masters, the *grammatistes* (to be distinguished from γραμματικός, used in a higher sense), the *citharistes*, and the *pædotribes*. It is said that at Sparta the education in reading and writing was not thought necessary, and there have been long discussions among the learned whether the ordinary Spartan in classical days was able to read. We find that Aristotle adds a fourth subject to the three above named—drawing, which he thinks requisite, like

---

[1] [ὦ φίλε παῖ] Θεωδώρηον μάθε τάξιν Ὁμήρου
ὄφρα δαεὶς πάσης μέτρον ἔχῃς σοφίας.

music, to enable the educated man to judge rightly of works of art. But there is no evidence of a wide diffusion of drawing or painting among the Greeks, as among us; and the same may be said of swimming on the gymnastic side, though the oft-quoted proverb, μηδὲ νεῖν μηδὲ γράμματα—*he can neither swim nor read*—has led the learned to assert a general knowledge of swimming, at least at Athens.

Later on, under the learned influences of Alexandria, and the paid professoriate of Roman days, subjects multiplied with the decline of mental vigour and spontaneity of the age, and children began to be pestered, as they now are, with a quantity of subjects, all thought necessary to a proper education, and accordingly all imperfectly acquired. This was called the *encyclical education*, which is preserved in our *Encyclopædia* of knowledge. It included, (1) grammar, (2) rhetoric, (3) dialectic, (4) arithmetic, (5) music, (6) geometry, (7) astronomy, and these were divided into the earlier *Trivium*, and the later *Quadrivium*. But fortunately this debasement of classical education is far beyond our present scope.

§ 33. The boys started very early for school, attended by their pædagogue, and appear to have returned for late breakfast. We may conclude from the Roman custom, though we have no positive evidence, that the afternoons were devoted to recreation, or the lighter gymnastic exercises. The later theorists speak much of pauses and of variation in study, but though we know there were a good many isolated holidays, we hear of no period of rest for both masters and boys, such as there must have been in the Roman dog days. There is something humane and affecting in the dying bequest of Anaxagoras, who gave his native city, Clazomenæ, a property on the condition that the anniversary of his death should be kept as a general school holiday. There were also special days of school feasts, such as the *Hermæa* and *Museia*, so elegantly described at the opening of Plato's *Lysis*.

§ 34. From the accounts we have of the teaching of the alphabet, as implied in Plato's *Cratylus*, and described by Dionysius (the rhetor) in illustrating Demosthenes' eloquence, it was not carried on in an analytical, but a synthetical way. Children were not taught words first, and then to analyse them, but started with individual letters, then learned their simplest combinations, and so on. Nor is this method ever likely to be supplanted by the other, at least in the case of stupid children. But we do hear of one curious attempt to make the alphabet an agreeable study in the so-called *grammatical tragedy* of Callias, about 400 B.C. This was the time when (in the archonship of Eucleides) the newer Ionic alphabet of twenty-four letters was introduced, and apparently ordered to be used in schools. The work of Callias was accordingly a poetical kind of A B C book, in which the single letters in turn spoke the prologue. The choral parts seem to have been refrains working out the simpler combinations of vowels with each consonant. The seven vowels were also introduced before the schoolmaster as female characters. But more we do not know, and it is probable that the book was only called *tragedy* from its external form, not from any plot.[1] The use of mnemonic verses to help children was no doubt as old as education; but we should have been glad to know the divisions of letters followed by Callias; for up to the times of the Sophists there was no proper analysis of the alphabet, and it is to them that we owe such studies as Plato's *Cratylus*, which, though sound as to the alphabet, is wonderfully childish as to etymology. Still the popular knowledge of 400 B.C. must have been a long way behind the *Cratylus*.

From the acquisition of letters, the child passed to the study of *syllables*, and we find *syllabising* used generally by the Greeks for elementary instruction in reading. But while the Greek child was not afflicted, like English children, with the absurd conundrums of a perfectly irrational spelling; while he had a fair guarantee that the individual letters reproduced the sound of the whole word, there were other difficulties in his way. He had not, indeed, to burden his memory with the sounds to be attached to symbols like *though* and *tough*, *plague* and *ague*, but he must, on the other hand, study with peculiar care the separation of words—interpunction—and also punctuation and accent. Accent, indeed, and the subtle use of the numerous particles, were given, and could only be given, by familiarity with Greek as a mother tongue. As Aristotle remarks, one could always know a foreigner, however well he spoke Greek, by the use of the particles. I heard Ernest Renan make the very same remark about foreigners' French a

---

[1] All our evidence, with every possible surmise about it, may be found in Welcker's *Kleine Schriften*, vol. i. p. 371 sq.

few years ago. But in classical days, accents were not even written, and words were not separated, neither were clauses distinguished by stops. Hence the difficulties of reading were considerably increased, as anyone may prove for himself by taking up a mediæval Greek MS. There, indeed, the accents are a guide, but even with them the separation of words is a difficulty, and has led to endless mistakes in our printed texts. We know, too, that the Greeks were particular about melodious intonation, and rythmical balance of clauses, even in prose : all this gave the *grammatist* ample scope for patience. There is even a special teacher—φωνασκός—mentioned in early days as regulating and training the singing voice of children. Indeed, we are surprised at the general assumption among their educators that everyone had both natural voice and ear.[1]

Thus reading aloud and recitations from the great poets attained a double object : the schoolboy was taught to enounce accurately and read rythmically ; he was made familiar at the same time with the choicest extracts of the best masters in the older literature. I have already spoken of Homer ; but the Lyric poets, like Tyrtæus, and the Gnomic, like Theognis, were also largely used at school. Indeed, it is not a little remarkable how many of these old poets were themselves called schoolmasters. This school use gave rise to *Chrestomathies*, or selections

---

[1] This assumption may perhaps hardly seem surprising when it still prevails among the English public as regards girls. Accordingly, a vast amount of time and brain power is wasted in the endeavour to make them play and sing, though nature has peremptorily precluded it in most cases.

of-suitable passages; and there are many critics who think that our present texts of Theognis represent such a selection. The golden verses of Pythagoras, the many collections of proverbs, or *maxims* (ὑποθῆκαι), point to the same practice. Written books were still scarce, libraries very exceptional, and thus the boy's education was far more prosecuted by dictation and by conversation than nowadays. Without doubt this made them less learned, but more intelligent and ready, than we are; and there are even in the days of Hellenic decay complaints of the increase of books, of the lust after much reading and various lore.[1] We are told that in Sparta and Crete all children learned hymns to the gods, and metrical statements of the laws, to be sung to fixed melodies; and this (if a fact) has justly been called a political as well as religious catechism.

§ 35. It was very late in the history of Hellenism that any mention of the learning of foreign languages meet us. Even in the wide studies pursued at Alexandria, no systematic course in languages is ever mentioned, and people still had recourse in international business to those who happened to be born of mixed marriages, or by some other accident had been compelled to acquire a second tongue. There is indeed much curious evidence that the Greeks, being really bad linguists, found great difficulty in acquiring the Latin tongue, even when it became the language of the rulers of the world.[2] Strabo[3] notes that

---

[1] The objections of the Eleatics and Platonists to the moral side of Homer and the other epic poets will be discussed in connection with the philosophic attempts at reform in higher education.

[2] Plutarch (*Life of Demosth.* 2) laments his inability to master Latin, and the difficulties it presents when not acquired very early.

[3] iii. 4. 19.

whenever historical treatises were composed in foreign languages, they were inaccessible to the Greeks, while the Romans did nothing but copy partially and imperfectly what the Greeks had said—a remark which might now be sarcastically applied to the relations of German and English philology. This Greek inability to learn, or contempt of, foreign languages reminds us of the French of to-day, whose language, until lately, held the place in Europe which Greek held in the Roman Empire, when every respectable person knew Greek, and when the Senate were able to receive and treat with foreign ambassadors speaking in Greek.[1] We have above noted the danger actually threatening that children might learn Greek so early and exclusively, as to speak their native tongue with a foreign accent—a state of things which the Romans would have resented strongly in their rulers —in that respect widely different from the English people of to-day. Thus the Romans attained, what the Greeks missed, the opportunity of learning grammar through the forms of a foreign language.[2]

§ 36. When the children came to writing, we must not imagine them using ink and paper, which was far too expensive. Instead of our slate they used tablets covered

[1] Up to the mission of Carneades and his fellows (B.C. 155) an interpreter had been necessary.
[2] This seems to me a very important point, and I do not know how our training of boys in the strict and clear Latin grammar can ever be supplied adequately by any other means, though I have one great and recognised authority—Mr. Thring—against me, who thinks that boys should learn the logic of grammar through English analysis.

with wax, on which the pointed stylus drew a sharp line, which could be smoothed out again with the flat reverse end. There were double lines drawn on the tablets, and the master wrote words for the boys to copy. We are told that he at times held the hands of beginners in forming letters. Quintilian suggests that the letters should be cut deep in a wooden tablet, so that the child could follow them without having his hand held; and it was in this way that the Ostrogoth Theodoric managed to sign his name, by having a metal plate pierced with it, which he then laid on the paper, and stencilled out the letters. There are on the walls of Pompeii many scribblings of boys, evidently repeating their school exercises; and in Egypt was found a tomb with a set of wax tablets, all containing the same verses of Menander; but one of them a model, the rest copies varying in excellence; and under some of them the approving judgment *diligent* (φιλοπόνως). This curious set of relics, in the possession of Dr. Abbott, of New York, is apparently the school furniture of a master buried with him.

§ 37. There is no reason to think that the average Greek attained anything like the fluency in writing which we now consider necessary. Plato[1] says it is only necessary so far as to be able to write or read; to write fast or elegantly must not be attempted within the range of ordinary education, except in rare cases and with peculiar natural gifts. Indeed, as slaves did all the copying work, and as published books were always in their handwriting, there may have been the same sort of prejudice against a

[1] *Laws*, 810—if the *Laws* be indeed Plato's.

very good, clear hand which many people now feel against an *office hand*. At Athens there was a special officer, γραμματεύς, to write out, or direct the writing out of, public documents; there was also a ὑπογραφεύς, a *secretary* to *take minutes* (ὑπογράφεσθαι) at public meetings. Besides the formal writing in separate capital letters, which we have on so many inscriptions, and which was probably the hand taught to children, there was a cursive hand, which we see in the Greek papyri of second century B.C. found in Egypt. In later MSS. we even find a regular shorthand, exceedingly difficult to decipher.[1] The lines were drawn, especially on wax, with a little coin-shaped piece of *lead* (μόλυβδος), and the drawing of lines appears to be called παραγράφειν. Instead of the sharp metal or bone stylus, a *reed* (κάλαμος), like our pens, was used on papyrus or parchment with ink. Quintilian prefers the wax and stylus, because the constant dipping in the ink distracts and checks thinking—a curious objection, and worth quoting to show the difference between his age and ours. But when the new stylograph has been used for some time, we will no doubt find men asserting this of the old-fashioned pen and ink.

§ 38. The school commentary, or explanation of the poems or other literature thus written out, was probably quite elementary. Grammar only began to be understood by the Sophists, and we have specimens of exercises on the use of the article, and on the question of genders, in a very comic dialogue in Aristophanes' *Clouds*, where the pupil of the new school ridicules the ignorance of old

[1] Cf. Wattenbach's specimens in his plates of Greek MSS.

Over-training in Mother Tongues. 61

Strepsiades. It is likely Prodicus' work *on the correct use of language* (ὀρθοέπεια) gave a great stimulus to this branch of education. But we cannot argue that these studies of the mother tongue which make our use of it more conscious than before, had any better effect on prose writing or on conversation than the very parallel studies of English which have of late years invaded or infested all our schools. Good breeding and natural refinement seem the natural (and are probably the only) safeguards of a mother-tongue in its ordinary use, and there is even great danger that a conscious analysis of idioms may banish from the writing of a language many valuable and characteristic turns which are based upon a more subtle propriety than that of school logic. Fortunately, local dialects have a great power of resistance. The Warwick or the Galway peasant will speak their own accents, and even use their idioms, in spite of all compulsory teaching of English grammar in the schools; but the reducing of all written English to one standard (both in spelling and in idiom) is like the reducing of all written Greek to the *common dialect*—a very great loss and damage.[1]

§ 39. We pass to the teaching of elementary science.

[1] If we had phonetic spelling, our dialects would be preserved, as the various Greek dialects were, or as the Italian now are, and thus the history of our language in the present day might become possible to ourselves and our descendants. As it is, we are concealing from all enquiry this most interesting subject—I mean the varying pronunciation—by our absurd artificial spelling, and we are banishing local idioms by stamping them with the mark of vulgarity. This latter is the natural and right consequence of having classical models. But had we possessed the older dialects in phonetic writing, our standard would have been widened, like that of the Greeks, to include important provincial varieties.

Geometry was still an advanced study, and though in high esteem among the Greeks, as one of the most elegant and perfect, seems not to have been taught in schools. Arithmetic was regarded either as the abstract *science of numbers* (ἀριθμητική), and as such one of the most difficult of sciences, or as the *art of reckoning* (λογιστική) to be employed in the ordinary affairs of life. Mercantile Greeks, like the Athenians and Ionians generally, among whom banking was well developed, must have early found this a necessity; but even in Greek art, architectural perfection was attained by a very subtle and evidently conscious application of arithmetical proportions. This was first shown in the accurate measurements of the Parthenon by Penrose, and was no doubt expounded in the treatise written on this building by its architect, Ictinus. In the great temple of Zeus, at Olympia, the use of multiples of 7 and 5 has been shown so curiously applied by an American scholar that he suspects the application of Pythagorean symbolism by the architect Libon. But of course this was ἀριθμητική in the strict sense, and is only here mentioned to show how the Greeks must have been led to appreciate the value of the science of numbers. Ordinary schoolboys were taught to add, subtract, multiply, and divide, as they now are, but without the advantage of our admirable system of notation.

§ 40. Starting from the natural suggestion of the fingers—a suggestion preserved all through later history by such words as πεμπάζεσθαι (literally, *to count by fives*, but used of counting generally)—the Greeks represented num-

Arithmetical Notations.

bers by straight strokes, but soon replaced ||||| either by a rude picture of a hand V (as we find in Roman numbers), and made two such symbols joined together to represent 10 (X), or else the higher numbers were marked by the first letter of their name, viz. M and C, in Latin *mille* and *centum*. So in Greek X (χίλιοι), M (μύριοι), &c. The smaller numbers were represented in ordinary counting by the fingers of the hand, not merely as *digits* (a suggestive word, in itself a survival of the process), but according as they were bent or placed, fingers represented multiples of 5, and so were sufficient for ordinary sums. Aristophanes even contrasts[1] this sort of reckoning, as clearer and more intelligible, with reckoning on the abacus, or arithmetical board, which has still survived in our ball-frames. We are told that the fingers were sufficient to express all figures up to thousands, which is indeed strange to us; but both the finger signs and the abacus failed in the great invention we have gained from Arabic numerals, the supplying of the symbol o. The abacus used in Greek schools appears to have had several straight furrows in which pebbles or plugs were set, and at the left side there was a special division where each unit meant 5. Thus, 648 (DCXXXXVIII) was represented in the following way:—

		M
o	o	C
	o o o o	X
o	o o o	I

[1] *Wasps*, 656 sq.

This abacus was ascribed to Pythagoras, but was in all probability older, and derived from Egypt, where elementary science was well and widely taught from very early times. When initial letters were used for numbers, as Π for πέντε, and Δ for δέκα, combinations such as ΔΙ meant 50. Last of all we find in our MSS. a system of using the letters of the alphabet for numbers, preserving ς (ἐπίσημον) for 6, and thus reaching 10 with ι, proceeding by tens through κ (20), λ (30), &c., to ρ (100), σ (200) and for 900 using ↗. This notation must not be confused with the marking of the 24 books of Homer's epics by the letters of the alphabet, and was borrowed directly from the Phœnicians, as the Hebrew system shows.

Further details as to the technical terms for arithmetical operations, and the progress to be attributed to a nation using so clumsy a notation, must be sought in professed handbooks of antiquity.[1]

As regards geometry, all we can say is that in the days of Plato and Aristotle both these philosophers recognise not only its extraordinary value as a mental training, but also the fact that it can be taught to young boys as yet unfit for political and metaphysical studies.

Having thus disposed of the severer side of school education, we will turn to the artistic side, one very important to the Greeks, and suggestive to us of many instructive problems.

[1] These are the ordinary terms: adding = συντιθέναι, προστιθέναι; subtracting = ἀφαιρεῖν, ὑπεξαιρεῖν, Latin *deducere*; multiplying = πολλαπλασιάζειν, and the factors πλευρά, a geometrical conception, as in the second book of Euclid; dividing = μερίζειν: no general word for *quotient* is found.

CHAPTER VI.

THE SUBJECTS AND METHOD OF EDUCATION—DRAWING AND MUSIC.

§ 41. It is likely that most writers on Greek education have exaggerated the importance and diffusion of drawing as an ordinary school subject. Even in Aristotle's day it was only recognised by some people—probably theorists,[1] and Pliny tells us that it was Pamphilus, Apelles' master, who first had it introduced at Sicyon, from which it spread over all Greece. These combined notices point to its not being general before the days of Alexander. But the theorists recognised its use and importance earlier, first and most obviously for critical purposes, that men might better judge and appreciate works of art ; secondly, for that æsthetical effect which is so forgotten by us, the unconscious moulding of the mind to beauty by the close and accurate study of beautiful forms.

The usual word ζωγραφία for painting, and ζωγράφος for drawing-master, suggests to us that *figure drawing* was the early and the principal branch of the art known and taught. From the earliest times rude figures had been scratched and coloured on vases, and the number of vase

---

[1] ἔστι δὲ τέτταρα σχεδόν, ἃ παιδεύειν εἰώθασι, γράμματα καὶ γυμναστικὴν καὶ μουσικήν, καὶ τέταρτον ἔνιοι γραφικήν.—*Pol.* viii. p. 259.

painters in historical Greece must have been so considerable as to disseminate some general feeling for the art, though we hear of no amateur vase-painting, such as is in fashion among ladies of our own day. On the other hand, landscape painting was of late growth and very imperfect development. The prominence of sculpture, even polychromatic sculpture, made its absence less felt. Owing to the old Greek habit of personifying nature, and expressing every mountain and river by its tutelary gods, we find in the great pediment sculptures of the best epoch that curious indication of the landscape by its tutelary gods—looking on calmly and unconsciously at the action of the principal figures—which is perhaps the most peculiar characteristic of all Greek art. Thus the local rivers, the Alpheus and Cladeus, are represented lying at the ends of the great eastern pediment of the temple at Olympia, witnessing the combat of Pelops and Œnomaus with no more expression of feeling than the landscape which they represent would manifest.

The earliest essays at landscape proper were, moreover, not rocks and trees, or that wild country which the Greeks never loved, but buildings and artificial grounds, with regular lines and definite design. The first attempt was made to satisfy the requirements of the theatre, and the fact that scene-painting and shade-painting (or perspective) were used as synonymous terms shows the truth of the report that Apollodorus (*circ.* 400 B.C.) first discovered the art of representing the straight lines of a building in depth, by a departure from that *orthography* in geometrical drawing which had hitherto been practised.

Drawing Lessons.

If we may judge from the many sketches of this sort of suburban landscape which are preserved on Pompeian walls, the proper knowledge of perspective was not even in later times diffused among ordinary artists, whose figure-painting on these walls is in every respect vastly superior. On the other hand, the figure-painting on vases of the best epoch is so conventional that we can hardly believe Greek boys were taught to draw figures with a proper knowledge of living or round models, and must assume the drawing lessons to have been chiefly in geometrical designs.

According to Ælian, there were maps of the Greek world to be had at Athens, and therefore presumably in schools, when Alcibiades was a young man; but this isolated notice, backed up by one or two allusions in Aristophanes, must not be pressed too far. The confusion between the terms for drawing and for writing utensils arises from the same materials being used in practising both—as if we used the pencil only in learning to write. The same *stylus* (γραφίς) which was used for writing on wax tablets was used for drawing outlines on the same, and the earliest training in drawing, if we may trust the statement of Bötticher, was the copying of the outlines of models proposed by the master.[1] After firmness had been attained, delicacy of outline was practised, and ultimately a fine paint, which was used to paint black and red outlines on white tables, or white on black.

[1] Ὑπογράφεσθαι is the technical term for this drawing of models.

§ 42. Though the diffusion of drawing was late and doubtful, this was not the case with music, in its strictest sense. For its importance was such as to make it a synonym for culture in general, and to leave us doubtful in some cases whether Greek authors are speaking in this wider or the narrower sense. But it is from music proper that they all would start, as affording the central idea of education.

Here is one of the features in which Greek life is so different from ours, that there is the greatest possible difficulty in understanding it. When modern educators introduce music into boys' recreation time, and say it has important influences in humanising them, though in this they may approach the language of Greek social reformers and statesmen, they mean something widely different. The moderns mean nothing more (I conceive) than this, that the practice of music is a humane and civilising pursuit, bringing boys into the company of their sisters and lady friends, withdrawing them from coarse and harmful pursuits, and thus indirectly making them gentler and more harmless men. It is as an innocent and social source of amusement that music is now recommended. Let us put out of all account the far lower and too often vulgar pressure on girls to learn to play or sing, whether they like it or not. For here the only advantage in view is not the girl's moral or social improvement, but her advancement in life, by making her attractive in society. Such a view of musical training is quite beneath any serious notice in the present argument.

What has above been said will be considered a fair

statement of the importance given to music by modern thinkers. And accordingly, when we find all Greek educators and theorists[1] asserting a completely different kind of importance in music, we find ourselves in presence of what is strictly a historical problem. It is not enough for the Greeks to admit that martial music has strong effects on soldiers going to battle, or that doleful music turns the mind to sadness in a solemn requiem for the dead. They went so far beyond this as to assert that by constantly playing martial music people would become martial, that by constantly playing and singing passionate and voluptuous music, people became passionate and voluptuous. Consequently, the proper selection of instruments of music and of words became a subject of serious importance. The flute was cultivated at Athens till Alcibiades spurned it for distorting his handsome face, and caused it to go out of fashion at Athens. But this aversion to the Bœotian instrument was supported by the theorists on the ground that it had no moral tendency, that it was too exciting and vague in the emotions it excited; also that it prevented the player from singing words to his music.

But when we would infer from this that it is really the text, and not the actual music, which has the mental effect—when we are disposed to add that in our own time

---

[1] Aristotle implies in his discussion (*Pol.* book vii. 1) that there had arisen in his day radical critics who asserted that music was merely an amusement, with no other importance. But he sets aside this opinion as hardly deserving of refutation, seeing how strong was the consensus of opinion against it.

instrumental music is a higher and more intellectual kind of music, which has no moral effects save good ones, and that it is the libretto of the opera, or the sentiment of the song which does harm—the answer from the Greek point of view is conclusive against us. Though much stress was laid upon the noble words which were sung, the music was known to have the principal effect. Plato in a celebrated passage even inveighs bitterly against the gross immorality and luxuriousness of all mere instrumental music, which admitted so much ornament, so much exaggeration of expression, so much complexity of emotion, as to be wholly unsuited to his ideal state. It is indeed perfectly true that the intellectual effort in understanding instrumental music, at least some instrumental music, is far greater than is required for appreciating, or imagining one appreciates, a simple song. To understand a string quartet of Mendelssohn, or still more a symphony of Beethoven, is an intellectual task far exceeding the abilities of nine-tenths of the audiences who hear them.[1] But apart from all such intellectual strain there is a strong, though indefinable passion about this very music, which has the deepest effects on minds really tuned to appreciate it.

If this be too subtle an instance, there is another so striking, that it is worth mentioning on the chance of the reader's verifying it some day for himself. The Hun-

---

[1] Aristotle fully appreciates this, and admits, even in his perfect polity, popular music to suit the vulgar listener, who cannot understand what is really classical (*Pol.* viii., ὁ γὰρ θεατὴς φορτικὸς ὤν, κ.τ.λ.).

garian gipsies who form the national bands are chiefly occupied at entertainments in playing for the national dance—the *czardás*—tunes which have now become familiar—some of them—through the transcriptions of Liszt and Johannes Brahms. The dance consists in a gradually increasing excitement, starting from a slow and grave beginning. The change is produced merely by increase of time in often repeating the same air,[1] and also in adorning it with flourishes, which are added *ad libitum*, and somewhat barbarously, by the members of the band according to their taste. The effect of this gradual hurrying and complicating of the same tune is inexpressibly affecting to the mind. It represents excitement, and often voluptuous excitement, to the highest degree. It would have thoroughly shocked Plato and his school.

This simpler example, though less easily verifiable to the English reader, is really more to the point, for there can be no doubt that it is owing to the increase of complication, and the growth of the intellectual combinations in music, that we have lost sight of what the Greeks thought so vital—the direct moral effects of music.

§ 43. The question remains, What did the Greeks convey by this theory? Were they talking nonsense, or was their music so different from ours, that their theories have no application in our day? We cannot adopt either of these solutions, though all our researches into Greek scales, and into the scanty examples of tunes still extant,

---

[1] In some cases a very florid adagio is succeeded by a lively plain tune in galop time.

are unable to show clearly what they meant. We cannot make out why tunes in the Doric scale—a scale varying slightly from our ordinary minor scale—should be thought manly and moral, while Lydian measures—a scale like our ordinary major scales—should be thought immoral.[1] We must give up the problem of finding out a solution from the Greek scales. But this we may fairly assert, that our music, being directly descended from the old Church scales, which again were derived from the Greek, cannot be so totally different from that of the old Greeks as to warrant the inference that theirs could be moral or the reverse, and ours indifferent to morals. We may depend upon it that they did not talk nonsense, and that the general consent of all their thinking men on this curious point is well worthy of our most serious attention.

It is probable that the far greater complexity of our music, the multiplication of instruments, the development of harmony, has brought out intellectual instincts unknown to them, and so obscured the moral questions once so striking. The Chinese of the present day, who have a music far simpler than ours, mostly on the tetratonic scale, are said to speak of the moral influence of music as the Greeks did, and to put the composing and circulating of tunes under a certain control. They used to have state composers charged with this duty, in order to preserve and improve the morals of the people.

[1] Some people have thought these scales only indicated differences of pitch. This is false, or rather a misapprehension, because in a fixed set of notes—like the white notes in our pianos—various *kinds* of scales could only be found by starting higher or lower. But how could a mere difference of pitch affect morals?

Moral Dangers of Music. 73

Although then it seems that the simpler the character of a national music, the more clearly its moral effects are perceived, we only want a closer analysis to detect the same qualities in our own composers. Much of the best music we now hear is unduly exciting; it feeds vain longings, indefinite desires, sensuous regrets, and were the evidence stated in detail, the sceptical reader might be convinced that here we are far behind the Greek educators, and that we often deliberately expose our children to great moral risk, by inciting them to express their semi-conscious desires in affecting music. The majority who have no soul for music may be safe enough (though this is not certain); but those whose soul speaks through their fingers, or their voice, are running a very serious danger, of which there is not the least suspicion among modern educators. To seek corroboration from the characters of leading musicians were invidious, but not without instruction.[1]

[1] It is not difficult for a man who has devoted sufficient time to music, and has known many musical people, to find some analogy to Dorian, Phrygian, and Lydian modes, as moral agents, in our modern music. For surely the real meaning, the real depth, in the art is this: that it represents, and by representing stimulates within us various emotions. Like all the other faculties of man, the emotions are a great class of mental phenomena improved and strengthened by a certain quantity of stimulus, but exaggerated and injured by being overstrained, or too perpetually exercised. And it is the peculiar province of music to awaken emotions too subtle and various for the coarser utterance of words, and therefore to fill the mind with feelings delightful indeed and deep, but from their very nature unutterable in words, and inexplicable except by sympathy. You cannot convey to an unmusical man what is called the expression of an air, that is to say, the emotion it has caused within you. Let us add that if it could be explained, it would not have

This enquiry is no digression which requires apology. It is a point in which we do not seem to have reflected the distinctive value which it really possesses. It is this very feature in the question which has caused the moral effects of music to be wholly overlooked in a cold and logical age, when many men are not affected by it, and in which everything inexplicable by direct statement is likely to be considered unreal.

The emotions, then, which it is the proper object of music to stimulate, are of that subtle character, that they cannot be defined. Different composers will no doubt excite a different *complexion* of feeling in the mind. The works of Haendel and J. S. Bach produce a thoroughly satisfied and cheerful temper, even when they treat sad subjects, whereas Beethoven has almost always about him that profound melancholy, which is to a mind in distress more sustaining in its sympathy than all the comfort of consolation. But this only describes the general character of the emotions produced, and not the emotions themselves. For these are often not consciously before us at all, but influence us, like our prejudices, from a hidden vantage-ground within the soul.

But, alas! the history of this delicious stimulant is like that of all the rest. Men begin to crave for it, and then constantly pursue it; they will not be satisfied without stronger doses, and presently even these cease to have their effect, except by intoxication. In such case the stimulant is no longer applied to exciting an emotion, but to satisfying a passion. And this latter differs from the former in being more violent (being perhaps compounded of several emotions), and in containing some coarser bodily element either consciously or unconsciously.

It may be illustrated from what are called sentimental songs. If we compare the old chaste love songs that are found among the national melodies of England, and still better of Ireland, with the love songs in one of the greatest of modern operas, Gounod's *Faust*, the distinction will be easily apprehended. When an Irish girl puts sweet wild music to the words of her song, and is then better satisfied with it than if she merely spoke it, the reason is this, that there are in her love a number of tender emotions, far too subtle to be uttered in the words, but which are conveyed in the expression of the melody. The very same may be said of the as deeply as the ancients, and which is well worth discussing without pedantry or sentimentality. It is also true that the general aspect of this side of Greek education is more interesting and fruitful than the enquiry into the structures of the particular instruments they used —an antiquarian question very minutely discussed by learned historians of music, and by compilers of archæological lore. On these details we may here be brief. The subject has been exhausted by Mr. Chappell, our best historian of music.

§ 44. In education we never hear of the use of those more complicated instruments, such as the τρίγωνον or *harp*, the double flute and others, which were used by professionals. On the other hand, the favourite syrinx, or Pandean pipe, was only in fashion among shepherds and not in schools. We may assume that nothing was there admitted but the simplest form of stringed instrument, the *lyre* (λύρα), which was originally made by stretching strings across the inside of the back shell of a tortoise. These shells are often to be found dry and clean in river courses through Greece. The tortoise when dead is eaten out by ants, or other insects, the shells separate, and are carried away and cleaned by floods. This most primitive kind was, however, supplanted by a more elaborate form,

solemn, almost religious love songs of the old Italian composers, in which knightly reverence for the gentler sex is so apparent. Let the soberest critic compare this music with the splendid duet in the garden scene of Gounod's *Faust*, and more especially with the concluding song of the act (that in six flats). Expressive this music is beyond description, and expressive of love, but how different!

which used the two shells of the tortoise, and fastened, in the position of its front legs, a pair of goat's horns, which were spanned near their extremity by the ζύγον, or yoke, to which strings were drawn from the far end of the shell, over the nether surface, or breast shell, which was flat. This, with seven or at most ten strings, was the ordinary instrument used to teach Greek boys to play. The more elaborate cithara, which still survives, both in name and structure, among the Tyrolese, was a lyre with a sound box built of thin wood, or metal plates, and elongated into hollow arms (where the lyre only had horns, or solid wooden arms), so that the resonance was considerably greater. This in the form called πηκτίς had fifteen or more strings, and does not here concern us. The use of the bow for stringed instruments was unknown to the Greeks, but they used for playing the *plectrum*, which is still used by the Tyrolese for their *zither*.

The favourite wind instrument was not our flute, which was called πλαγίαυλος, or 'cross-played aulos,' and which was not popular, but our clarinet, the αὐλός, which was held straight, was wide at the mouth, and produced its tone by means of a vibrating tongue in the mouthpiece. The ordinary aulos was played without any artificial aid, but for the double aulos, where two reeds of different pitch were blown from the same mouthpiece, a leather bandage was tied over the player's mouth, into which the mouthpiece was fitted. This was the most extreme form of that disfigurement of which the Greeks complained in flute playing.

The tunes taught to boys are now lost, and we cannot

Ugliness of extant Tunes.

hope to reproduce them. But there is good reason to think that they would not suit the developed taste of our day, and would be considered dull and even ugly. This we may infer from the few extant fragments of Greek tunes.

CHAPTER VII.

THE LAST STAGE OF EDUCATION—MILITARY TRAINING OF THE EPHEBI.

§ 45. THE small size and narrow bounds of Greek states made the support of a professional army seldom possible, and accordingly we find expedients now suddenly again become fashionable from very different causes—a citizen army, and general liability to military service. No Greek boy was allowed to pass from his school days into citizen life without some preliminary training and practice in the use of arms, and in military discipline. This is the discipline of the *ephebi*, or grown-up boys, concerning which so much has been written of late years by the learned. A number of inscriptions regarding the duties and ceremonies to be performed by them have been lately discovered, and we seem to see in them a sort of general agreement throughout Greece, rather differing in the time allotted and in other details, than in principles.[1] There were actual masters in the art of using arms, so far as this was not included in the gymnastic exercises of the palæstra; we do not hear, however, of much drilling, and probably the drill of Greek armies, if we except the Spartans, was very

[1] Cf. the list in Grasberger, iii. 65.

imperfect in the best period. It was not until the growth of mercenary armies, and (almost simultaneously) the great military outburst at Thebes under Epaminondas, that war became a science in our sense.

On the other hand, all the patrol duty of the frontier was done by these *ephebi*, who, at about the age of sixteen, were brought into the rank of citizens by a solemn service and sacrifice, at which they swore oaths of fidelity and patriotism, and undertook their military duties as a preliminary to their full life of political burgesses. The orphans of citizens killed in battle had their arms and military dress presented to them (at Athens) by the State. The youths assumed the short dark grey *cloak* (χλαμύς), and the broad-brimmed soft *hat* (πέτασος), suitable for marching duty, and then, as περίπολοι, or *patrolling police*, they looked to the safety of the country, the condition of the roads, and occupied the frontier forts, of which we see such striking remains still in Attica. The mountain fort of Phylæ, that of Dekelea, of Œnoe (or Eleutheræ), of Sunium, of Thorikos, of Oropus, and others, were the stations from which the frontiers were patrolled.

It is doubtless owing to this precaution, that though we read of insecurity in the streets of Athens by night, we never read of brigandage through the country. Some scholars have indeed asserted that the περίπολοι had police duty to perform in the city, and at the public assembly. This we need not accept, though on solemn occasions, and when a great ceremony was to be held, they appeared, not only to preserve order, but to participate in the show. It is the latter duty which we see them performing in the famous friezes of the Parthenon, which represent the Panathenaic procession. They were allotted a separate place in the theatre, and were in every respect regarded as a distinct order in the State, the hope and pride of their city, and its ornament on all stately occasions.

Their patrol duty on the frontier was appointed to them for divers reasons. They attained through it the discipline of arms, and learned some of the hardships of campaigning. They learned an accurate knowledge of the roads and ways through their country, and of the nature of their frontier, and that of their neighbours. They were kept away from the mischiefs which threaten youths of their age in every city.

But the Athenians and other Greeks were careful not to commit the mistake of which we now hear so much—that of expecting these youths under twenty to face the enemy in battle. They were specially reserved for garrison duty, and one of Myronides' victories was particularly noted, because he fought it with these boys, who were not expected to stand firm in the horrors of a battle.

§ 46. According to the words of the oath, indeed, as preserved by Stobæus and Pollux, the standing firm beside one's comrade is specially mentioned; but even if this interesting document be not spurious, as Cobet supposes,[1] this particular declaration may be considered prospective, and applying to the remainder of the citizen's life. I add the words here for the benefit of those who

[1] *N. L.* p. 233.

have not the Greek text at hand: 'I will never disgrace these hallowed weapons, or abandon my comrade, beside whomsoever I am placed, and I will fight for both sacred and common things personally and with my fellows: I will not leave my country less, but greater and better by sea and land, than I may have received it: I will obey the rulers for the time being, and obey the established laws, and whatsoever others the commonwealth may agree to establish; and if anyone abolish the ordinances or disobey them, I will not allow it, but will defend them personally and with the rest. I will obey the established religion. Be my witnesses Aglauros, Enyalios, Ares, Zeus, Thallo, Auxo, Hegemone.' Though Cobet be right that some features of this oath can hardly have been generally used through the course of Athenian history, and that it is probably made up at a late period, the list of gods, so curious and unlike what a late pedant would invent, points to some old source, and perhaps there are other really historical traditions in it.

The *general* authenticity of this text has rather been confirmed by the discovery of the oath of the ephebi of Dreros (near Knossus) in Crete—an inscription of undoubted authenticity. Here, there are not only the general declarations of loyalty and patriotism, but special oaths to support the allied Knossus, and declarations of hatred and hostility against the town of Lyttos.[1] This formal declaration of hatred may be compared with the outspoken aristocratic oath quoted by Aristotle: 'I will

---

[1] Cf. for the text of this oath *Philol.* for 1854, p. 694, or Grasberger, iii. 61.

be ill-disposed to the demos, and will do it whatever harm I can devise.'

The various religious ceremonies connected with the admission to the status of an ephebus, which was considered distinct both from a boy and from a man—the sacrifices, the cutting of the long hair (except in Sparta), the solemn assembly of relatives, remind us strongly of the *Confirmation* of the Christian Church, to which it is the heathen parallel.

§ 47. What a solemn procession of ephebi must have been is best shown by the equestrian and sacrificial procession on the frieze of the Parthenon. We notice some young men naked, some in the short cloak and hat, riding horses and leading victims. The riding of the horses was not so easy as with us, for, in the first place, they had no saddles and stirrups, and in the second it was thought necessary for a good display to have the horse continually on his hind legs. A quiet walking horse in a procession was thought very tame by the Greeks. Hence the management of these curvetting and caracolling steeds must have necessitated careful training in their riders. Again, we find others leading bulls to the sacrifice, and the frequent mention of contests with bulls has even misled many authorities to imagine that the Attic ephebi practised bull-fighting. The fact is that an unruly victim was of evil omen, and hence the careful leading of these beasts, with skill and strength combined, so as to make a proper part of a great show, came under ephebic training. This, too, we see on the Parthenon frieze. Wherever, in fact, any public display was required, the artistic taste of the Greeks ordained that the fairest and most stalwart men should be there to adorn it; and as nothing is so beautiful as a crowd of vigorous fresh youths, in the bloom of life and the happiness of youth, we can conceive how splendid was a State procession then compared with those of our day, when the grandest show is one of old generals, effete officials, and other venerable but decrepit magnates, who must be covered with fine clothes, brilliants, and orders to prevent their real ugliness and decay from being painfully obtrusive. In Roman days we hear of these youths being employed as guards of honour when distinguished foreigners visited Athens.

§ 48. Though this ephebic training is spoken of as universal, and it seems that after his inscription into the *register* (ληξιαρχικὸν γραμματεῖον) of his deme, which was his patent of citizenship, every Athenian lad was bound to serve as *patroller* (περίπολος), and undergo his military training, there must have been many exceptions, and indeed this whole education is evidently that of the higher classes, and unsuitable for the poor. In Roman days, we even find strangers coming to Athens and enrolling themselves among the ephebi, as those wealthy foreigners who understand what culture means often send their sons to England to receive the unique training of the English public schools. But this points to its being a privilege, a special and much prized education, though we do not know what restrictions there were, or how the sons of poorer men, who could not afford the time and outlay, avoided it. The number of official ephebi was never, I fancy, large, and always a class from which Pheidias might well select for his models, when seeking for ideal types of youth and manliness.

It has indeed not been sufficiently noticed in the various essays on this ephebic training, that the very idea of such a class never occurs in Herodotus, or in Thucydides, though it does in Xenophon;[1] and if Plutarch speaks of Alcibiades influencing the *ephebi* in the gymnasia with his wild schemes of western conquest, we may be sure the historian transferred the titles and notions of his age to older times. In the third century B.C. there are so many inscriptions about this class extant, that it must have assumed a most prominent place in Attic life. From that time onward into Roman times, we hear of it constantly, and from many sources. It is impossible that Socrates and his school should not have alluded to it, had it already formally existed. We may therefore infer that though its component parts—the formal enrolment and sacrifices at a certain age, the patrol duties, the gymnastic and musical training, the procession duty at festivals—were developed in the best period of Attic history, their official reduction to a state system of education could not have taken place till later, till the decay of practical public life had given men time to theorise about methods of restoring by education what was irreparably lost.

Apparently the earliest *formal* notice is in a fragment of the orator Lycurgus, who, in his famous speech on his own management of the Athenian exchequer,

---

[1] Especially in his *Education of Cyrus*.

Ephebic Organisations.

alluded to the statue of a certain Epicrates, which had been set up in bronze *on account of his law about the ephebi*. We cannot tell whether this was a special enactment or not. But it *may* have been the very law which established this famous system, so praised and sought after by all the Hellenistic world in Roman days. If so, the establishment would date from the very time when it proved of little real importance to the history of Attica or of the world.

Nevertheless, the many inscriptions reveal to us certain curious and interesting features, which make us approve of the good taste of Cicero and his friends, when they sent their boys away from Rome to Athens, as we send our sons to schools in England. Thus the learned Germans, who have investigated with great pains the various titles of the magistrates or dignitaries among these ephebi, are often at a loss to determine whether they are masters set over them, or leaders among the ephebi themselves. Indeed, the so-called ἄρχων τῶν ἐφηβῶν—*head of the ephebi*—appears to have been no other than the most successful and brilliant youth, the representative and spokesman of the rest, like the senior prefect at some of our public schools. No doubt, learned men who, in future ages, investigate the ephebic training of the English, will puzzle themselves over the senior prefect at Winchester, and wonder whether he was a master or a boy, and if a boy, how he could have so much power entrusted to him. We also find that the expenditure of keeping up the solemn processions and public contests was so great, that the ephebi themselves were encouraged to contribute largely; and if they were rich, they gained an importance disproportionate (we may suspect) to their age. What is even more interesting to English students is that they had independent clubs and associations, and even held solemn meetings, where they used the terms of public life, and entitled the *resolutions* (ψηφίσματα) enacted in their *assembly* (ἀγορά) *laws—νόμοι*. They had archons, strategi, agoranomi, and even areopagites in these associations of youths. It must have been with the approval of these formal meetings that the gymnastic side of the ephebic training became gradually discredited. Whether the dislike of great generals like Alexander and Philopœmen to athletics contributed to change public opinion we cannot tell. But I confess to feeling a considerable sympathy with the reform which asserted the superiority of hunting and riding to the exercises of the gymnasium—a change which is regarded by some German critics as a melancholy sign of degradation.

§ 49. In these later days, when the seven subjects of knowledge, including rhetoric, philosophy, &c., were formally adopted, the ephebic training assumed the character of an university course. There were indeed masters appointed for fencing, the use of arms, dancing, and wrestling, as of old; but the leading philosophical schools did not then carry off the youths from the ephebic training, they rather supplied it with formal professors. In the better and strictly classical days, before we hear of the technical term *ephebi*, the practical training of the youths for patrols, and then as incipient citizens, rather corresponded to what we call the sixth form at a public school, and did not embrace really philosophic teaching, such as is supposed to be found at our universities. It had the same mixture of the physical and intellectual, the same attention to mere accomplishments, the same careful surveillance which we practise in schools, but which is not a complete introduction to full citizen life. This was the summit of Spartan training, where the object was not to train really political men able to discuss public affairs and assist in the government of the State, but brave soldiers, and fine men, physically able to endure hardship and submit to strict discipline. Something quite different and intellectually higher was needful for a really democratic life, for an intelligent understanding of State functions, and the proper discussion of them. It was all very well to dance complicated figures with grace, to play the lyre and sing sweetly with it, to wrestle and run with force and ease. This was the old training, which made fine soldiers, but good citizens only in the sense of stupidly ignorant, and therefore obedient, hearers of the orders of their superiors. The necessity of a change came with the rise of democracy in Greece, and the Greeks provided themselves, when the need arose, with teachers suited to their wants. These men, the sophists, were the first who gave any education corresponding to our university courses, and to these we now turn.

CHAPTER VIII.

HIGHER EDUCATION—THE SOPHISTS AND SOCRATES.

§ 50. As everyone knows now, the real position and merits of the Sophists were first brought to light by Grote in his monumental *History of Greece*. Since the publication of that book the English scholar has learnt that sophist in early Greek history is not synonymous with liar and villain, undermining public morals and sapping religion. Within the last few years the influence of this new view is gradually reaching the Germans, a nation not very ready to adopt, in philology at least, English opinions. But this very natural reluctance has its exceptions; for in the most important new book on the history of Greek philosophy, Zeller's last edition, we find that, in spite of sundry reservations, the main results of Grote's investigations are recognised and adopted.

Before I go on to appropriate from these authors that part of their account of the Sophists which belongs properly to the subject of Greek education, it is worth reflecting a moment on so very remarkable an instance of misunderstood evidence as this controversy exhibits. The main body of philologists simply followed like a flock of sheep Plato's and Aristotle's polemic against their own rivals. Plato inherited from Socrates a strong antipathy to these practical and often utilitarian teachers. But it was for the most part the same sort of antipathy that the solid university professor of our own day has for the successful crammer. The competition mania of the present day has created a demand for these specialists, who do not profess anything more than their special trade of passing men for examinations, and who do it admirably, and derive from it large emoluments. So the rise of democratic institutions, and the spread of international debates, made the fifth century B.C. in Greece one that required suddenly a set of practical teachers for men who practised at the bar or debated in the public assembly. We are too much in the habit of thinking that such men required training merely in rhetoric—in the way of disputing and of plausibly stating their views. They required more, they required education in general subjects, and of course not a deep education, but such an one as would enable them to talk intelligently, and make and understand allusions to the deeper questions of the day. We hear that now in America it is not an uncommon thing for men who have risen suddenly in the world, and for their wives, to send for a teacher and say : 'I am now in a position to move in educated society, and to be required to speak on public affairs. My early training was entirely neglected. I want you to instruct me in the ordinary topics of the day, as well as in those points of art and science which may be serviceable for my purpose.' And such instruction, very superficial, no doubt, and inaccurate, but highly practical, is often given.

§ 51. Now let us imagine that an intelligent Greek or other foreigner, totally unacquainted with modern journalism, were to seek for evidence of its moral value and the real benefits it confers upon us. What answer would he receive? If he applied to the journalists themselves, they would tell him that it was their object so to furnish their readers with all the current topics of instruction, as to make them able to converse intelligently without any further study. They would also profess to be leaders of the moral sense of the public, praising what was of good repute, and blaming the wicked, exposing abuses, and expounding virtue. They would also claim the merit of supplying the public with arguments in favour of a disputed conclusion, so that men might be furnished with weapons to meet their intellectual adversaries. He would naturally ask, on hearing this exalted programme, whether all this was done out of pure philanthropy, or with any ulterior view, more especially, whether there was any pecuniary gain attached. They would reply that they did indeed take money for their teaching—and the labourer is worthy of his hire—but they would appeal to any of their readers whether the instruction afforded was not greatly in excess of their remuneration. With this reply our stranger might perhaps be but half satisfied, and might have some suspicion that independent evidence would not come amiss; and on enquiring from thoughtful men what emoluments were to be gained by this profession, he would hear that, if successful, it was one of the most lucrative known, and that many of the contributors confessedly worked, not for the sake of conviction, but of gain. He would next enquire whether success was always in their case a test of solid merit, and would discover that however it might be so intellectually, from a moral point of view such was not the case. The most thoughtful and candid members of our society would explain to him that, here as elsewhere, men delighted more in reading what fell in with their prejudices than what exposed them, and that by pandering to this defect, and following in the wake of public opinion, newspapers often succeeded better than by honest and fearless teaching. He would hear that almost every paper belonged to some political party, whose errors and weaknesses it felt bound to justify and protect; furthermore, that for the sake of clearness and of brevity, as well as from a want of care to do more than please for the hour, many arguments in the daily papers were superficial and illogical, not clearing but obscuring the real questions at issue. He would certainly, therefore, in the course of his enquiry, come to look upon them as a class or profession; but yet, if he spoke of them as such, he might be surprised to hear himself corrected by the journalists or by their friends. They would deny that they were a distinct profession, and say with truth that *all* intelligent men who desired to teach were to some extent journalists, who are marked by no fixed principle, by the bonds of no special education. Even their own critics, he would hear with surprise, at times joined them and wrote to instruct the public. They were a class and not a class, a profession and not a profession, with a common object, to some extent a common method, but hardly any common principles, any direct co-operation, any common interest to outbalance their jealous rivalry.

§ 52. Is this a fair picture of the moral side of journalism? It is obtained simply by describing, in the wake of Plato and of Mr. Grote and of Sir Alex. Grant, the old Greek Sophists. These then were really the Greek journalists, who, before the days of posts and printing, carried about from city to city the latest news, the most recent criticism, the most modern views of politics and of education, the newest theories on morals and on religion. It may be thought irreverent to compare St. Paul to our daily press, but I cannot better explain myself than by pointing to that most graphic scene in the Acts where the apostle arrives at Athens. He is seized by the eager and curious public, as we seize the precious journal in some remote country place when we have been separated from the current of affairs for a few days. And no doubt they first asked him what local or political information he had brought from his previous sojourn, just as we first read the messages from Paris or London; and when this curiosity was satisfied, they began to enquire what more he had to say; and finding that he was an ethical teacher or sophist, they proceeded at greater leisure to enjoy the rest of his communications, just as we should turn on to the leading article, the correspondence about Ritualistic innovations, or the reviews. St. Paul was taken for a Sophist, and justly so in some sense, for he taught morals and religion; still more, he taught a new religion. We all know how far he differed from that class. Flippant, plausible, ingenious, sceptical, they were the idols of the public, but the aversion of those deeper minds, to whom the ignorance and prejudice of the masses are not a source of material gain but rather a grievous and galling spiritual burden.

§ 53. This is what the Greek Sophists really were, crammers not for special competitions, but for the general requirements of higher society, and of political life. They crammed more or less honestly, more or less efficiently, for a generation or two. Then the want of them passed away, as we may hope the want of the modern crammer will pass away with the superstition that we can find out practical merit by mere examinations. At Athens and throughout Greece the encyclopædic teaching of the Sophists was presently carried into minute speciality by teachers of rhetoric, of dialectic, and of morals, just as the professors of geology of thirty years ago are being supplanted by special teaching in fossil anatomy, botany, and mineralogy. From the middle of the fourth century B.C. the Sophists disappear as a class altogether. It is nevertheless certain that they left no bad name behind them in Greece, except among the immediate followers of Plato and Aristotle, for in the second century A.D. the title was revived as one of the highest honour, and attaching to the greatest literary post in Athens.

We need not assert that these teachers were as strictly business-like as the modern *coach*, or that they confined themselves as strictly to their definite object. They often boasted of great performances which were beyond the reach of ordinary people, and were merely meant for display. But then their aims were far wider and more varied than those of the coach, and were not to be tested by the clear and definite result of the examination lists. Hence Plato and Socrates found it easy to pick holes in their programmes, and to accuse them of getting money under false pretences. These philosophers went further, and reviled them for taking money at all, bartering their wisdom for gold, and imparting virtue for a fee. All this was mere jealous polemic, and based on an unfair estimate of the attempt made by practical men to supply a public want. Yet even though Plato himself paints the leading Sophists as most respectable men, though we know from independent evidence that they were so, whether Plato confessed it or not, the attacks on the profession made by him and by Aristophanes—the one a radical reformer, and the other a blind conservative—have so imposed upon the learned that they have completely mistaken the real evidence on the question, and set down the arguments for the prosecution as if they were a judicial charge or a mature verdict. So powerful is the influence of literary skill, when it causes the survival of a single work amid the loss of all its fellows. Because Plato is our leading witness on the Sophists, because Aristophanes' satire has survived, men imagine that this must be the general verdict, and set down the bias and the prejudice of an individual as the reflex of public opinion.

§ 54. These men really shaped out the first form which university education took in Europe, meaning by university education that higher general training which, coming after school discipline, prepares men for the duties of social and political, as well as scientific and literary life.

General Type of Sophists. 95

In the city life of the Greeks, when residence in any foreign place entailed great inconvenience, it was evident that this university teaching could not occupy a fixed place. It was not till the amalgamation of the Greek nation under Roman sway that Athens became (like Alexandria) strictly an university town. So, as the students could not gather round the early sophist, he was obliged to go to them, wandering through Greece, and staying for a considerable time in each great centre, where the native youth could profit by him. But even in early days there were some enthusiastic pupils, who abandoned home and country, and wandered about as aliens in the wake of these brilliant teachers. The latter generally made high display of their acquirements, and gave exhibitions of eloquence and of argument to show the value of their wares. They lived an ostentatious life, like the professional artists of the present day, and though they made large profits, saved but little money. Their first object was to make ready and practical citizens, men able to collect and express their thoughts and give sound advice on public matters. For this purpose they not only taught the art of rhetoric, and that of disputation, but they were obliged to enter upon some of the great theories which form the basis of all practical life, the problems of philosophy, of ethics, and of religion. As we might expect, they took in all these an utilitarian view, such as a practical crammer would take. Some of them, such as Gorgias and Protagoras, studied philosophy deeply, but only to show that a devotion to metaphysic or to abstract science was idle, all knowledge being subjective, and varying with the age. Man was the measure of things; abstract nature was mere nothing. On the more pressing question of morals, though practically sound enough, and though some of them, such as Prodicus, were celebrated as moral preachers, they denied all immutable morality, and were content with obeying the existing laws of society, without admitting any permanent scientific basis for them. It was Socrates who first applied his great mind to solve this question, and his classes of young men—he was in this a regular Sophist or university teacher, and was commonly so called—were specially exercised in seeking for the permanent and immutable ideas implied in our moral terms which characterise our moral actions. As regards religion, seeing that the Greek faith had grown up in myths and poetry, and was embedded in an elaborate polytheistic mythology full of immoralities and absurdities, the Sophists were, as we might expect, sceptical, and so far opposed to the conservative public. One of them, Protagoras, actually professed his unbelief in the national faith, and was persecuted accordingly; others, though more cautious, and regarding any formal denial of transcendental truths as hardly practical, were justly suspected of agnosticism, as their moral essays kept suspiciously clear of theology. They were regarded as unsound in faith, and hence alleged to be unsound in morals by the orthodox, whose faith the Sophists charged fairly enough with the same objection.

§ 55. So the education of the Sophists came to be regarded by the soberest part of the public, the steady-going old people, as subversive of ancient and venerable traditions. In religion it was supposed to suggest, if not to teach, infidelity; in politics and society, radicalism. This is exactly the sort of charge we hear made by the old-fashioned public against the Universities —still more in Germany, where the gulf between the average and the learned part of society is far wider than it is here. When we University teachers make young men think, even though carefully avoiding (as we are in honour bound) anything which may shock the traditions in which they have been brought up, the mental agitation produced must nevertheless lead them to reject at least some superstitions which they have accepted on weak evidence. If our education does not produce this result, it is not worthy the name. But this partial and cautious scepticism is of course identified by the older generation, who are less spiritually developed, with the rejection of vital truths. And there are many cases where the young sceptic really oversteps his just bounds, and becomes as rash in negation as his fathers were uncritical in affirmation. Let us add that the orthodox party are not very particular about evidence, and will start a calumnious charge against a teacher whom they suspect and fear, with very little care about really proving their case. This party are, moreover, always supplied with powerful allies by the jealousies and differences among the teachers themselves, the elder and less able of whom often try to sustain their waning influence by an alliance with orthodoxy, and make up by theological popularity what they have been unable to attain for want of intellectual force and sympathy.

All these things, which now happen constantly in our Universities, are the exact counterparts of what happened in Greece in the days of the Sophists. They taught clever young men such surface knowledge of science as disgusted the deeper experts, and, what was more, they taught them that the experts were pursuing a vain shadow, and attempting insoluble problems. They taught them to avoid becoming specialists, and to apply themselves to public life. Just as the English Universities can boast of many great politicians and literary men, rather than of specialists in the sciences, and as they might hold that to produce a Gladstone or a Cornewall Lewis is better than to produce a Faraday, so the Sophists made general culture their professed object, and so far quarrelled with deeper philosophy.

§ 56. The same sort of proceeding in morals brought them into contact with Socrates, whose daily teaching may be regarded as the best university teaching of the day. Socrates was in all external respects a Sophist, and commonly regarded as such. He did not indeed travel about, being luckily a citizen of the largest and most enlightened city in Greece. He despised, too, wealth and ostentation of the ordinary kind, though he made himself no less remarkable by his voluntary poverty. But in more important respects, in despising abstract science and speculative philosophy, and sifting traditional theories of morals and society, in radically shaking up and often upsetting all preconceived notions, Socrates was a Sophist, and one of the most dangerous of them. He sought indeed to do what they had not done, to find some better and surer positive basis for morals, but the negative part of his work was far the most successful and striking. Hence the conservative public at Athens not only suspected and disliked him, but at the prosecution of their mouthpiece, Anytus, a most respectable and earnest man, condemned him to death, when he showed clearly that no verdict of theirs would restrain him from pursuing his occupation. This sentence on Socrates, which the orthodox party at Athens never regretted, and even justified, should indeed be a warning to those who calumniate their fellows in the interests of orthodoxy. But with this we are not now concerned.

The higher teaching of the Sophists and of Socrates, which was at best desultory, passed into the hands of successors like Plato and Isocrates, who established regular schools, and subjected their pupils to a regular course of training. This was all the more necessary, as the training given by Socrates had no definite limits, and his tendency was to keep young men talking and discussing ethical problems when they ought to have turned to practical life. Leisure was indeed in such high repute among the old Greeks that idleness was not reprehended as it should have been. The orthodox party made this objection with much force to the school or following of Socrates. In the case of Plato there was a regular course of higher philosophy, and his principal pupils became in their turn philosophic teachers. But the school of Plato was even more than that of Socrates an university training, for which there may even have been a matriculation examination, if we adopt literally the statement that no one was allowed to enter without knowing elementary geometry. The great fault of Plato, as of Socrates, was that he did not introduce men to public or practical life, but made them philosophers or idlers. In science, indeed, this special training was of great service, and the history of geometry would have been very different without these speculators. But the Platonic pupil when completely trained was professedly, according to the master himself, disinclined to join in politics, and only to be persuaded by his sense of duty, and the willing obedience of the public.

It is on account of the same sort of exclusiveness, even monastic in its strictness, that the famous brotherhood of Pythagoras deserves but a small place in any general history of Greek education. Admission to this brotherhood was only obtained through a strict noviciate, and the object of it was to combine peculiar religious asceticism with an aristocratic policy, and a sort of club life antagonistic to ordinary society. We have unfortunately only few authentic details concerning this sect, and know it best from the few echoes of it in early, and the many in later, Platonism. But it too may be regarded as a higher intellectual or university training, combined with collegiate life and its restraints, thus anticipating in spirit that feature which makes the English Universities so peculiar among the modern seats of learning in Europe.

I will return to Plato and his followers when we come

The Leading Sophists.

to consider the theories of education which the philosophers based on the phenomena of Greek history. And before we pass from the Sophists to the Rhetors, and show a further specialising of higher education in that direction, we may say a word in conclusion on the external history of these once celebrated, and since much maligned, educators. We hardly know them at all, save through their enemies, the specialist philosophers and specialist rhetoricians, and what we hear of them must be distrusted and sifted accordingly. Nevertheless, even from their enemies, we learn that the three greatest of them —Protagoras, Gorgias, and Prodicus—were eminently respectable and respected men. So was the fourth in importance, Hippias, though the encyclopædic pretensions he put forth to practise all trades and manual dexterities, as well as philosophy, history, and rhetoric, have left an unpleasant impression against him. Nevertheless, he was honoured at Elis, his native place, as their leading citizen, and compiled for them the annals of their famous past, in such a way as to gain universal acceptance.

As regards the other three, though they all professed to impart general education, and to give their pupils that negative training in philosophy which would arm them against false theories, yet they were each remarkable for some special line. Protagoras, apart from his famous philosophical position of the relativity of knowledge to him who knows, openly professed to teach *political* wisdom, and despised all other kinds of knowledge in comparison with it. Gorgias, on the other hand, though he wrote a famous treatise with the very Hegelian title 'concerning nature or the non-existent,' devoted his main attention to *rhetoric*, and was truly the father of technical Greek oratory. For though we hear of Corax and Tisias in Sicily, and of Empedocles, as having cultivated the art, the first recognised theorist and practical speaker was Gorgias. He not only delivered set speeches, but so trained himself as to deliver elegant discourses on any proposed subject, apparently without preparation, but of course with the help of a clever system of well-arranged commonplaces, which he applied with quickness and variety. The philosophy of Prodicus was chiefly ethical, and his apologues were very popular and quoted in after days. But more important were his *grammatical* studies, whereby he fixed the parts of speech, and laid the groundwork of the grammar of the modern languages of Europe. Indeed, the strict attention to form shown by all the Sophists led them to study language with peculiar care, and they were the forefathers of modern philologists in this as in some other respects.

A great many more Sophists are known by name, some of them depicted or maligned in Plato's dialogues, such as Thrasymachus, Polus, Euenus, but they do not present to us any special features. All are said to have insisted on the dictates of society as superior to any supposed law of nature, and this Hobbism has brought upon them the anathemas of moralists. Within the century 470-370, B.C. their part was played out, and even Plato in his later works no longer thinks them worthy of refutation.

CHAPTER IX.

THE RHETORS—ISOCRATES.

§ 57. It is argued by many scholars, who believe all that Plato says literally, and who think that the dark pictures of Thucydides apply only to his own day, and not to previous generations, that the Greeks were so degraded and debauched by this sophistic tampering with religion and morals, by this scepticism in philosophy, and by the rise of radicalism in politics, as to present from this time onward (430 B.C.) the symptoms of a decaying race. The Athenian State, in particular, is supposed to have lost its splendour and its seriousness, and to be now a mere mob-rule, far removed from the democracy tempered with despotism, which make it so great under Pericles. This view, which is strongly urged, for example, in Curtius' *History of Greece*, is based altogether on the complaints of Plato and Aristophanes, and the impression produced by the history of the aristocratic Thucydides, by Xenophon, and by the plays of Euripides. This is not the place to refute the theory generally, as has been done by Grote, who shows that never was the Athenian democracy so enlightened and moderate in policy as in the period after the close of the great war (403 B.C.). But in the particular department before us, that of education, we have already seen that this period after the Peloponnesian war is exactly the period when the sophistic higher education began to be discarded as superficial and even morally questionable, and the task of training the keener and more ambitious youth passed into the hands of greater specialists, either philosophers like Plato and his followers, or rhetoricians like Isocrates and Antiphon. Socrates forms the connecting link between the Sophists and the philosophic schools. Isocrates is hardly such a link, though he professes to be the philosopher in the guise of a rhetorician. Though he inveighed against his rivals the Sophists, he is hardly to be distinguished from them save in his being fixed at Athens, in his avoidance of displays (from natural inability rather than from choice), and in his declared conservatism in religion and politics, as contrasted with their scepticism. It is not just that the eminent respectability of Isocrates personally should be urged as another difference, when we adopt the fair view of the high characters of the leading Sophists. Isocrates, whose views are fortunately preserved in his own very diffuse advocacy of them, was strictly a university teacher, and so well recognised was this that *a pupil of Isocrates* meant something like our B.A. Oxon. For he had a regular course, and charged a considerable fee for his lessons. His pupils came from all parts of Greece, and stayed with him a considerable time. Moreover, he could boast that the most famous public men had been educated by him, and owned his influence in after days. This higher education he called *philosophy*, and he only differed from other professed Sophists (he says) in the modesty of his promises, and his distinct admission that he undertook merely to improve natural talent, not to change a stupid and ignorant youth into a man of acuteness and power.

§ 58. There is an interesting passage in the speech in vindication of his life,[1] which gives so clear a view of the prevailing opinions about higher education at Athens that I will transcribe it freely :—

'The ordinary attacks made upon us are of two kinds. Some say that going to the Sophists for education is mere arrant imposture; never has there been any system of training discovered by which a man can become abler in speech or wiser in deed, since all who excel in these respects differ by nature from the rest of mankind. The other objectors concede that those who submit to this training become indeed abler, but in a bad sense, and coupled with moral loss; for when they gain power, they use it to injure their neighbours. I will now refute both these objections.

'First, let us consider the absurdity of those who decry all higher education. They revile it, indeed, as worth nothing, and mere deceit and imposture, but yet demand from us that our pupils, as soon as they come, should show a complete change, that after a few days' intercourse with us they should appear better in discourse and abler than their elders in age and experience; but if they stay one whole year they should all be perfect orators—the idle as well as the diligent, the common-

[1] Περὶ ἀντιδόσεως, p. 98 sq.

place as well as the gifted. This they expect from us, though we never have made such promises, and though it contradicts the analogy of all other kinds of training, in which results are acquired with difficulty, and each with a various measure of success, so that some two or three only out of all the schools of all kinds turn out thoroughly proficient, while the rest remain mere average amateurs. Accordingly the objectors are silly enough to demand from a training, which they call unreal, an influence unknown in the recognised instruction of all arts and sciences !   Our teaching, then, is discredited for accomplishing exactly what the other arts do.   For which of you does not know that many of those put under the Sophists were not imposed upon, as is alleged, but have become, some of them, real experts in public life, others able instructors of youth, and even those who chose to remain in private life more polished in manners than they had been, and more accurate critics of arguments as well as of most ordinary things?

How, then, can a pursuit be fairly despised which has produced such results? for do not all men confess this, that those are to be esteemed the most thoroughly versed in their art or handicraft who can make their apprentices as good workmen as themselves? Now, in philosophy this very thing has happened. For as many as happened on a genuine and sensible guide will be found to have such a family likeness in their way of expressing themselves, that anyone can tell they have come from the same trainer. This similarity of type is conclusive evidence of the method and system to which they have been subjected. So, too, any of you could mention fellow-pupils who, as children, were the most ignorant of their fellows, but as they advanced in age became far superior in good sense and in eloquence to those once far ahead of them.'

The orator goes on, with his usual elegant diffuseness, to make many other developments of the same leading idea, all of which might be used with hardly a word of change by anyone defending our university education against the vulgar objectors who think that vast sums of time and money are spent upon it, with little or no result. Nor is the good which he does claim for his higher education anything different from what our Universities could claim, apart from the material good of prizes and degrees.

§ 59. The peculiar position of Isocrates was that of opposition to both Sophists and philosophers, and yet of likeness to both. He joined the Sophists in urging sceptical objections to the subtle theories of the metaphysicians, and in commenting upon the small outcome of their elaborate speculations. He joined the philosophers in attacking the boastful claims of the Sophists, who pretended to teach everything. But he joined with the more practical side in putting a training in rhetoric—a training in style, above everything. There were many reasons why this should be the case with higher education at Athens. In an age when books were scarce, and a reading public small; when the power of publicism only existed for poets, and when all state affairs were settled by discussion either in the assembly or in private meetings—in such a society a power of clear and elegant utterance was the highest and best outcome of education. Nor could any man then be considered educated who lacked that power, just as nowadays no man is called educated who cannot write correct English, and furthermore the writing of elegant English is justly accounted to indicate a thorough and general culture. For we are such severe judges in this matter; everybody thinks himself in this so well able to appreciate beauty, and pick out defects, that a man who can pass through the fire of criticism unscathed must indeed be equipped with no ordinary preparation, and may be pronounced a really cultivated man. This will explain to us the enormous importance of rhetoric in Isocrates' system—an importance, perhaps, enhanced by his feeling that here he was really able to do great and unique service. He evidently depended on natural mother wit to suggest ideas to his pupils; he apparently assumed that they had learned the ordinary elements of culture at their primary schools. He trained them, so far as we know, in nothing but the careful arrangement of their materials, the smooth transition of their arguments, and the perfection of their choice and collocation of words. In this matter of style, Isocrates may be regarded as not only the greatest master that ever lived, but as the father of the periodic or oratorical style in all the languages of Europe. Demosthenes, Cicero, St. John Chrysostom, Massillon, Burke—all these immortal men have profited by the analysis of expression which, through Isocrates, first formed Greek prose, and through it the borrowed graces of those who followed Greek models.

§ 60. To enter into a closer description of this system would not be to discuss education, but rhetoric, and we must refer the reader to treatises on that subject. We need only here call attention to the intense *studiedness* of Greek eloquence, and how they attained their perfection in prose—not by those violations of propriety which now please our sated taste, and which, when violent enough, as in the case of Carlyle, even pass for thoughts, and are to many the index of deep originality in something or other—but by a close and perpetual adherence to rules, often of a trivial, generally of a minute kind.

It is very curious for us moderns to read the details of these things in the old rhetoricians. There is not an apparent touch of nature—a word emphatically repeated, a sudden break off, an angry burst, even a *don't you see*, or a *by Jove*, or a *dear me!*—in a Greek oration, which was not noted as a *figure of diction*, or a *figure of thought*, and brought under the discipline of rules. We are even told that Demosthenes composed his prose in rythm, and avoided the use of more than two short syllables together. Isocrates certainly made the law against hiatus, against closing a word and beginning the next with vowels, a law adopted by all the prose of his age. Thus the formal education in rhetoric must have been no light task for the pupils of Isocrates and the other rhetors, and writing or speaking good Greek a far stricter and more difficult thing than writing English which will pass muster with the critics.

§ 61. Still there is room for surprise that the *matter* of higher education, the ideas to be acquired, should have been introduced indirectly under the guise of preparation for public speaking. No doubt this was an artificial and unnatural order of things. To subordinate the matter of knowledge to the form is always a mistake. But we may at least conceive the position of Isocrates' pupils if we compare it with that of the popular preachers, so powerful a generation ago, and even now playing no unimportant part in society. I have known more than one of these eminent men who educated themselves with great care generally, and in all directions, for the purpose of supplying themselves with matter for their discourses. And this is very well-meant, legitimate, and honest education, though perverted in order, and, like that of Isocrates, not likely to lead to really deep and thorough knowledge. We are told that in the present day there are people who read all kinds of books for the purpose of solving double acrostics, and I have heard men of intelligence advocate this foolish kind of riddles as promoting general education!

Thus the school of Isocrates stood side by side, and in rivalry, with the schools of Plato and Aristotle, as one in which elegance of form, and a superficial but graceful culture, were given to the higher youth, instead of the exact science and metaphysic which unfitted men for public life. It was a contrast somewhat like the Oxford and Cambridge type in England. Isocrates' own failure as a politician, and the little influence which his open letters on politics attained, made the wiser portion of men drift away still further from the sophistic aspect of his teaching, from the mixture of philosophy and politics with rhetoric;

Education in Later Days.

and so they again subdivided their training into the strictly rhetorical, such as had already been begun by Lysias and was carried out by Isæus, and the philosophical, for which an increasing number of schools now offered themselves. As the political power of Greece decayed, and its literary and artistic splendour became universally recognised, Athens became an educational centre to which youths from all parts of the civilised world flocked for their training. This later history of Greek culture will occupy us in our last chapter. But we must first give a brief account of the deeper theories of State education which Plato and Aristotle have left us, in contrast to the shallow popularity of Isocrates.

CHAPTER X.

THE GREEK THEORISTS ON EDUCATION—PLATO AND ARISTOTLE.

§ 62. It is usual in books on Greek education to give a very large space to the discussion of the *Republic* and *Laws* of Plato, and the *Politics* of Aristotle, because they contain elaborate and systematic recommendations as to the training of youth. But the States of both philosophers are ideal, Aristotle's not less than Plato's, and, though the educational portion of Aristotle's work seems fragmentary and unfinished, we cannot hold that any further developments would have brought it within the range of practical politics. Plato's notions were confessedly theoretical, and are discussed as such by all his commentators; but some scholars have given themselves endless trouble to find out how much of his system, especially in the tamer and less extravagant *Laws*, was borrowed from real life, and from actual states, as opposed to the creations of his own fancy. But in nearly every detail the distinction is purely conjectural. It is really for want of positive evidence that these theories have assumed such undue importance. To the philosophical theorist and the educational reformer the speculations of such splendid intellects in the early post-meridian of the glorious day of Greece must ever be most attractive and suggestive, but it is idle to transfer to a practical book, or to a historical account, what has never been realised.[1] These speculations, however, may fairly find a limited space here as showing what general effect the practical education already described had produced upon the most advanced thinkers of the day.

Unfortunately, we have here again only the aristocratic side, and that which would assert the State to be paramount and all-interfering through individual and private life. If we had the speculations of Lycophron and his school, who held, with truly democratical instinct, that laws were only useful to repress crime, and that the rest of the citizen's life was to be left free and uncontrolled, our notions about the theories of Greek education might be considerably modified. But, on the other hand, we have preserved to us the Hellene of the Hellenes; the school of Lycophron might only have recommended to us what we know by practical experience in modern society.

From the very outset Plato and Aristotle adopt quite definite principles. They assume that the State is to interfere everywhere and control the whole life of man. Thus the splendid Athenian democracy in which Plato lived had no power to wean him from his somewhat narrow prejudices. He despised the goods he possessed, and longed for a Spartan ideal, though its defects

[1] Few people have ever heard of the attempt to found a Platonopolis in Italy in the Renaissance times.

were plain enough before his eyes.[1] Still worse, the wide vista opened by Alexander into a larger fusion of ideas, and into widely various forms of society, had no power to emancipate the intellect of Aristotle from its ingrained Hellenic narrowness. It is necessary to make this strong protest at the outset, on account of the chorus of admiration sung by the pedants and pedagogues of modern days over these thoroughly unpractical and retrograde theories. One fact will speak volumes to the modern reader. Both of them look upon a small number of citizens, and indeed a small limit of territory, as essential to their schemes, no accurate or perpetual supervision by State police and direction being possible either in a great city or a large territory.[2] This will in itself show how antiquated they must have seemed even in the next century, when the Greeks woke to the ambition of ruling over kingdoms in the East.

§ 63. And yet there were some points on which these thinkers, especially Plato, were far more thoroughgoing than we are, chiefly from a total absence of that sentiment or sentimentality, which infects modern life. For

[1] Of course he saw and admitted these defects, but it is obvious that he thought them only defects of detail, which could be remedied by better arrangement; whereas the Athenian democracy appeared to him radically unsound. And yet could Sparta ever have produced such a splendid passage of history as the conduct of the Athenian army at Samos, when the news came (411 B.C.) that the constitution of their city had been overthrown, and an oligarchy established? Let the reader consult Grote's chapter on this.

[2] Plato even insists upon a fixed number, 11,080 men and the same number of women, all excess being guarded against either by exposing of infants or transporting adults into colonies.

Exposal of Children. 115

Plato, both in the *Republic* and the *Laws*, insists that education will be of little avail, if children are brought into the world deformed in body and warped in mind by the bad physical and mental condition of their parents. On some of these cases Greek society was agreed with him. In most states a deformed child was exposed, either to die, or to be picked up by some one who might run the risk of bringing it up to make a household slave.[1] For in most states, and certainly at Sparta, it would have been held a crime to propagate hereditary disease, and men were spared the disgusting spectacle of the scrofulous or deaf and dumb heir to a great name being courted in matrimony to perpetuate the miseries or the vices of his progenitors.

But Plato went further, and held that the production of the most important animal, man, should be regulated with even more care than that of the lower animals, in which such striking results have been obtained by artificial selection. He therefore recommended in his ideal State not community of wives—heaven forbid that we should follow Aristotle in repeating this gross

[1] The critics have shown that Plato gradually softened his recommendations on this point. In the *Timæus* he speaks as if he had never recommended exposal, but only a relegation of the children of unhealthy parents into his third grade of society. In the *Laws* (if it be indeed his work) he lets the whole matter drop, though it was to be expected that he should discuss it. Whether this arose from a gradual advance of humanity in Plato himself, or from the adverse criticism of the day, we cannot tell. The German critics (Zeller, Susemihl, &c.) hold the former. I am disposed to the latter, even though his successor, Aristotle, as they remark, is even more inhuman.

libel—but a careful State selection of suitable pairs, and their solemn union, under the guise of a direction from Providence by an appeal to the lot. These marriages were to take place at a fixed season, and all the children born of them within the year to be regarded the common children of all—here the word *community* may fairly apply. He has nowhere told us whether in successive years the same parents were to remain united, and hence we do not know whether his marriages were meant to be temporary or not. I fancy the point was of little importance to him. If the offspring turned out well, there would be no change; if badly, of course the guardians of the State would not sanction the continuance of an unwholesome union. Thus, though Plato was willing to allow sentiment its sentimental place, and to bring forward the decision of the rulers of the State as the will of Providence, marriages professedly arranged in heaven were to be permitted only with a strict view to the improvement of the race.

The objection that such an arrangement would destroy the sanctity and influence of the family, and thus abolish our most powerful engine of early education, was no objection to Plato. He wished to abolish separate families, and rescue children from the tyranny, the indulgence, and incompetence of individual parents, so as to put them under State discipline. And the State was absolutely nothing but one huge family, as far as the higher classes were concerned. To us who live in large kingdoms, who know that the family gives the law for individuals in ordinary life, and that schemes of public education cannot replace it, all systems which abolish the sanctity of the home are inadmissible.

§ 64. No point in Plato's scheme excites more sympathy nowadays with advanced thinkers than that of equalising the sexes in education, and subjecting women to the same training and duties as men. For he held that, though nature had not made women as strong as men, and that their important functions in the production of the race put them under some inconveniences and disabilities, there was, nevertheless, no reason to assume any permanent difference in kind. If such a theory is thought revolutionary by most people in modern society, what must it have been in the days and among the people of Plato's age! Here, again, what guided him was an exaggerated estimate of the liberty and importance of Spartan women, who when young were encouraged to exercise in public, and who, when married, maintained over their husbands an influence far exceeding that of women in other Greek households. But then we must not forget the small culture of the men, their devotion to military training, and the consequent necessity for women to use their own judgment in the management of their homes.

§ 65. On the other hand, if we may digress for a moment on account of the interest and importance of the subject, there is no valid reason why the physical production of the race should not receive infinitely more attention than it does, within the bounds of our present social arrangements. In the first place, though the sentimental reasons for marrying are still put in the foreground, and though at wedding speeches and in amatory correspondences some divine predestination, or the sentimental compulsion called falling in love, is assumed the only efficient cause of marriages, we know that many reasonable considerations intervene and are the real motives of action. These motives—the acquisition of wealth, or position, or connection; the desire of home comforts, and of a life independent of external amusements, a calm mutual respect—are commonly enough confessed even by the very people who parade sentimental reasons; and whenever a marriage appears suitable from rational considerations, no trouble is spared by match-makers to induce young people to imagine themselves drawn together by some subtle and sentimental affinity—like Plato's guardians, who were to pretend the providential lot as their guide.

If, then, such be the case; if even now there are civilised countries and classes of people who openly profess prudential reasons as the best for marrying, it will only require a better education of public opinion to enable men to advance to the position that the physical and mental vigour of the resulting children is a motive to be consciously considered in the selection. We may first reach the stage of avoiding all hereditary taint, as people now fly an infectious disease. Such avoidance would ultimately stamp out or reduce to a minimum this evil, and the race would escape a great part of the direst and most hopeless of its physical miseries. Then the systematic and deliberate desire that there should be healthy children will discover many conditions now unknown, when so many of our unions are the result of chance, or avarice, or, still worse, of passion. Men of science will begin to make observations on the difference of physical antecedents which cause such curious differences in children of the same house. And the day will come when, from a body of such observations, valuable practical rules may be deduced. We may thus improve our race as the Spartans did in old Greece, and they, we know, were perfectly successful in obtaining what they sought—a high average of physical strength and beauty.

All this, we may hope, will only be the introduction to a far more important, but far more difficult, problem—the determining of the conditions which produce genius. There is no reason to doubt that these conditions are mainly transient, for genius is no fixed heritage, the most splendid instances coming from obscure and ordinary parents. Nor does the mere combination of the suitable parents work its effect uniformly without other more limited conditions. For we find the great leaders of the world, sometimes the only child, sometimes eldest, sometimes youngest, or in the middle of a family of brothers and sisters as obscure as their parents. The careful observation, then, not only of the parents, but of the particular passage in their life which produced an intellectually splendid offspring, is one upon which we cannot expect light for a long time, and until people have become accustomed to regard the general improvement of the race of far greater importance than they now do. If such results could be obtained even approximately, if even in one case out of ten, intellectual excellence could be produced as we reproduce physical perfections, then indeed the perfectibility of mankind would no longer be a vague dream, but would show some signs of a partial fulfilment.

Are we to hope that such an advance in ideas will take place in our own day? We have perhaps advanced beyond the stage when men regard genius as distinctly heaven-born, and the direct gift of the gods, apart from any natural conditions. If it is indeed heaven-born, it is now conceded to be such through the combination of natural causes. But, on the other hand, our best and most refined people will recoil with deep aversion from making a scientific analysis of such conditions ; they will exclaim that the possible advantages are as nothing compared with the desecration of that mystery which has been hallowed by the sacraments of the Church, and protected from profane enquiry by a cloud of delicate sentiment. To reduce the holy estate of marriage to the deliberate and scientific production of conditioned offspring will destroy, say they, all the sanctity of the relation, and with it the purity and dignity of our homes.

These weighty and respectable objections are to be met by observing that it would be idle and wrong to attempt any reform in opposition to the unanimous sentiment of the very people who alone could carry it out— our most sober and refined classes. Until this sentiment can be gradually changed by argument, and come to be looked on as a ver.erable and amiable superstition, nothing will be accomplished. But it is a matter of history, that the most respectable and hallowed sentiments, if irrational, can be gradually removed by a progress in what Mr. Lecky calls *rationalism* or intellectual enlightenment. We can even now point to the important fact, that in those countries and those ages where marriages have been confessedly arranged from prudential reasons, they have not been less sacred, nor has home life been less pure, than where vague and irrational sentiments have been brought into the foreground. The lower class Irish are as faithful and happy in their homes, and the marriage tie is as sacred and honoured as it is anywhere in the world; and yet among them a love-match is rare. It is a matter of cows and of pigs, of the succession to a farm, nay, often of arrangement by the landlord for reasons of his own; and yet these marriages are as happy and as pure as if they had been the outcome of a great mutual passion. The same thing may be said of married life in the country parts of France, where a thrifty and provident race accommodate their unions to their circumstances, and leave the extravagances of great passion to poets and Parisians.

The history of Greece offers a more notable instance. If we ask where in Greece the home enjoyed the greatest honour and sanctity, where the house-mother stood highest in reverence and social importance, and where violations of fidelity were rarest, no one would hesitate to answer, at Sparta. Yet at Sparta all the sentiment, all the delicacy of the marriage tie was sacrificed to the duty of producing healthy children for the State. Plutarch tells us of a state of things which modern people would think wholly subversive of all purity, of old men ceding their rights of temporary unions and exchanges, for the sake of desirable offspring. The Spartan men and women were not wanting in sentiment about marriage, in advocating the honour and sanctity of the marriage tie, but their sentiment led them to regard a fine offspring as the noblest outcome of marriage, and one to which all other considerations were secondary. Hence it was in accordance with their sentiment that they adopted the same kind of precautions, as regards physical perfection, which a later and wiser age may adopt as regards intellectual and moral perfection.

This possibility of improving intellect by careful selection was beyond Plato's vision; he only thought of physical qualities in the arrangement of his unions. But it is one of the most remarkable points in his exclusive and aristocratic society that he makes provision for the adopting of any particularly bright child of the operative class among his guardians, so that they might benefit by the accident. The degradation of poor or unhealthy children of the higher class is also contemplated.

His arrangement of the years of education is as follows: It is divided into three parts. Beginning with the learning of proper myths and tales, it proceeds to easy gymnastic, followed by music and poetry, with reading, writing, arithmetic, and some elementary mathematics, all of which occupy from the seventh to the eighteenth year, and thus correspond to our schooling. Then comes military training up to the twentieth year—a division to which we, who have no conscription, have no analogy, as the Germans have. Next follows the second division of higher studies in pure and applied mathematics for ten years, and the third in metaphysic for five years. These are, of course, quite wide of any practical scheme, and are intended to form those philosophic rulers who will regard their whole life here as a preparation for a higher sphere.

§ 66. His views on the details of music and gymnastic were not materially different from those of the practical educators which we have discussed, save that he proposes to train his guardian class with more detail and circumstance than were possible for any ordinary public.

He is unpractical, and even absurd, in his curious prudery about the tales and legends which children are to learn. He objects to Homer, to the tragedies, still more to the comedies, and no doubt to the folklore of the day, as inculcating base and immoral views of the gods and their relations to men. Fairy tales are always to represent God as one and as perfectly good. He even goes so far —but here he can hardly be in earnest—as to recommend that children shall learn by heart his laws instead of poetry and myths![1] Throughout all his remarks on this subject, he evidently ignores the culture of the imagination as such, which we recognise as so important that we even tolerate or overlook immoralities or manifest fictions in aiming at this kind of amusement and culture of children. Indeed, it is certain that when children are taught fairy tales *as such*, the immoral acts of real life, such as robbery and murder, are only accessories to the imaginary life, in which there is generally some rude justice.

[1] This is in the *Laws*, of which the genuineness is not without doubt.

Even apart from this particular question, we find all through Plato's theory of education a very mischievous dislike of any liberty of opinion, or liberty of life, in the youth of his state. He goes so far in the *Laws* as to make heresy of opinion penal, and to punish with imprisonment those who will not conform to the doctrines of the lawgiver. If there be anything which would tempt us to reject the *Laws*, as not the genuine work of Socrates' disciple, it is this strange narrowness of view, which makes Grote argue that the actual Athens of Plato's day was superior to the ideal he constructed. But doctrinaires of all ages hate human liberty. Nor do the Greeks ever seem to have been forced by the pressure of circumstances to mark off the close of formal education by a fixed period, like our graduation at a university, when the young man is expected to strike out into the world, and henceforth educate himself in practical life.

§ 67. The educational book of Aristotle's *Politics* (VII. in the now received order) is a mere fragment, which suggests many problems, and solves but few. Even with the help of some important corrections from the *Ethics*, we find it the narrow and old-fashioned scheme of a pedant Greek, written with admiration for the artificial discipline of Sparta, and unable to understand even the far more splendid Hellenic ideal sketched by Thucydides in his speech of Pericles. We know, however, from the *Ethics* that he felt the essential importance of family ties between husband and wife, between parents and children. Hence he rejects Plato's proposal of abolishing the family, and insists that the ideal state must consist of households in the strict sense. But, on the other hand, he quite agrees with Plato's view that the social and moral aspects of marriage are by no means inconsistent with a strict supervision of the producing of healthy children by the State. He foreshadowed the state of things anticipated above, when husband and wife will still feel the deep sanctity and thorough loyalty of their relation, and yet not leave to mere accident the most important product, nay the only product, so far as the State is concerned, of their union. He is just as careful as Plato in recommending care of unborn children, by attention to their mothers' air and exercise. He is still more ruthless in advocating the destruction, either before or after birth, of illegitimate offspring. Neither can he, any more than Plato, imagine an ideal state capable of such expansion as to contain a great people, nor can he dispense with disabilities for most of its members, such as slaves and operatives.

He does not contemplate the very long and elaborate after-training of Plato's guardians, for he does not conceive this world as a preparation for another, but as an end in itself. And it is probably for this reason that he is so superior to Plato in analysing the function of refined recreation, and the ennoblement of leisure by æsthetic pleasures. Thus he sees that music is to be utilised as a recreation for youth, as well as for a moral engine of education. He has explained in his *Poetic* that dramatic poetry is not mere fiction, to be banished from the ideal state as teaching falsehood or depicting crime, but a representation of human life deeper and more philosophic than history, inasmuch as history only widens the intellect, while the drama also purifies the emotions of the spectator. It may even be argued that history widens the intellect only so far as it is conceived as a drama—a development of human character—and not as a mere recitation of facts.

While he does not enounce so clearly as Plato that gymnastics are mainly a training for the character, he sets his face against that physical training which studies nothing but the development of muscle, on the ground that if at all excessive it defeats its own object by engendering an unhealthy state, and that as we cannot work the body and the mind together with any severity, it must generally coincide with ignorance or with an illiterate life. Even the Spartan military training, which was opposed by them to athletic training, falls under his censure.

He will not concede with Plato the equality in kind of the sexes, but thinks the functions of women are distinct in kind from those of men, and therefore not to be perfected by adopting the same training. Thus he is on the whole tamer and more conservative, but also less suggestive, than his great master.

§ 68. The main value of his fragment on education is that it shows how thoroughly the subject had been discussed in his day. Thus, after determining that the civic side of the citizen is all important, and that therefore all education must be public and the same for all, as in Sparta, he proceeds thus with his argument:[1] 'What then is education, and how are we to educate? For

[1] vii. 2.

there is as yet no agreement on the point; all men are not of the same opinion as to what the young should learn either with a view to perfection or to the best life; nor is it agreed whether education is to aim at the development of the intellect or the moral character. Nay more, from the ordinary standpoint the matter is quite confused, and it is not clear to anybody whether we are to train in what leads to virtue, in what is useful for ordinary life, or in abstract science. All these alternatives have their advocates. Again as regards what leads to virtue there is no general consent, for since men do not agree in what they honour as such, of course they cannot agree about the training to obtain it. As regards what is useful for life, it is obvious that there are certain indispensable things which must be taught, and it is equally clear that there are others which must not. All occupations are divided into those which a free man should practise, and those which he should not, and therefore this affords us a limitation in the learning of useful arts.' He goes on to show that no trade is gentlemanly if it injuriously affects the body, or enslaves the mind by being practised for hire. Even the fine arts, if studied in this way, or professionally, are to him an unworthy occupation, and are only to be pursued in youth as a recreation or æsthetic training; so that in middle life men may be competent judges of such productions, and either better able to enjoy them (as in music), or less likely to be deceived (as in the purchase of works of art). Having applied these principles to athletics, about which he says little save in recommendation of moderation, and against any professional training, he turns to the question of music, on which we have already given the views which he held in common with the most serious Greek educators. On this subject, too, there was controversy. He has before him three theories: is it mere *amusement* (παιδία), or an engine of *education* (παιδεία), or an æsthetic *pleasure* (διαγωγή)?[1] Perhaps

---

[1] viii. 5, §§ 3-10: Περὶ δὲ μουσικῆς ἔνια μὲν διηπορήκαμεν τῷ λόγῳ καὶ πρότερον, καλῶς δ' ἔχει καὶ νῦν ἀναλαβόντας αὐτὰ προαγαγεῖν, ἵνα ὥσπερ ἐνδόσιμον γένηται τοῖς λόγοις, οὓς ἄν τις εἴποι ἀποφαινόμενος περὶ αὐτῆς. Οὔτε γὰρ τίνα ἔχει δύναμιν, ῥᾴδιον περὶ αὐτῆς διελεῖν, οὔτε τίνος δεῖ χάριν μετέχειν αὐτῆς, πότερον παιδιᾶς ἕνεκα καὶ ἀναπαύσεως, καθάπερ ὕπνου καὶ μέθης· ταῦτα γὰρ καθ' αὑτὰ μὲν οὐδὲ τῶν σπουδαίων, ἀλλ' ἡδέα καὶ ἅμα παύει μέριμναν, ὥς φησιν Εὐριπίδης· διὸ καὶ τάττουσιν αὐτὴν καὶ χρῶνται πᾶσι τούτοις ὁμοίως οἴνῳ καὶ μέθῃ καὶ μουσικῇ· τιθέασι δὲ καὶ τὴν ὄρχησιν ἐν τούτοις. Ἢ μᾶλλον οἰητέον πρὸς ἀρετήν τι τείνειν τὴν μουσικήν, ὡς δυναμένην, καθάπερ ἡ γυμναστικὴ τὸ σῶμα ποιόν τι παρασκευάζει, καὶ τὴν μουσικὴν τὸ ἦθος ποιόν τι ποιεῖν, ἐθίζουσαν δύνασθαι χαίρειν ὀρθῶς· ἢ πρὸς διαγωγήν τι συμβάλλεται καὶ πρὸς φρόνησιν; καὶ γὰρ τοῦτο τρίτον θετέον τῶν εἰρημένων. Ὅτι μὲν οὖν δεῖ τοὺς νέους μὴ παιδιᾶς ἕνεκα παιδεύειν, οὐκ ἄδηλον· οὐ γὰρ παίζουσι μανθάνοντες· μετὰ λύπης γὰρ ἡ μάθησις· ἀλλὰ μὴν οὐδὲ διαγωγήν τε παισὶν ἁρμόττει καὶ ταῖς ἡλικίαις ἀποδιδόναι ταῖς τοιαύταις· οὐθενὶ γὰρ ἀτελεῖ προσήκει τέλος. Ἀλλ' ἴσως ἂν δόξειεν ἡ τῶν παίδων σπουδὴ παιδιᾶς εἶναι χάριν ἀνδράσι γενομένοις καὶ τελειωθεῖσιν. Ἀλλ' εἰ τοῦτ' ἐστὶ τοιοῦτον, τίνος ἂν ἕνεκα δέοι μανθάνειν αὐτούς, ἀλλὰ μή, καθάπερ οἱ τῶν Περσῶν καὶ Μήδων βασιλεῖς, δι' ἄλλων αὐτὸ ποιούντων μεταλαμβάνειν τῆς ἡδονῆς καὶ τῆς μαθήσεως; καὶ γὰρ ἀναγκαῖον βέλτιον ἀπεργάζεσθαι τοὺς αὐτὸ τοῦτο πεποιημένους ἔργον καὶ τέχνην τῶν τοσοῦτον χρόνον ἐπιμελουμένων, ὅσον πρὸς μάθησιν μόνον. Εἰ δὲ δεῖ τὰ τοιαῦτα διαπονεῖν αὐτούς, καὶ περὶ τὴν τῶν ὄψων πραγματείαν αὐτοὺς ἂν δέοι παρασκευάζειν· ἀλλ' ἄτοπον. Τὴν δ' αὐτὴν ἀπορίαν ἔχει καὶ εἰ δύναται τὰ ἤθη βελτίω ποιεῖν· ταῦτα γὰρ τί δεῖ μανθάνειν αὐτούς, ἀλλ' οὐχ ἑτέρων ἀκούοντας ὀρθῶς τε χαίρειν καὶ δύνασθαι κρίνειν; ὥσπερ οἱ Λάκωνες· ἐκεῖνοι γὰρ οὐ μανθάνοντες ὅμως δύνανται κρίνειν ὀρθῶς, ὥς φασι, τὰ χρηστὰ καὶ τὰ μὴ χρηστὰ τῶν μελῶν. Ὁ δ' αὐτὸς λόγος,

we have dwelt too long on these theories, but it seemed desirable to give the reader the *locus classicus* on the Hellenic theory of music, which was discussed above (§ 43), and which, in spite of all our studies of Greek life, is still quite strange and incredible to modern theorists in education.

§ 69. There is yet another scheme of education left us by the classical age of Greece, Xenophon's *Education of Cyrus*, which, in the form of a very tedious novel on the life of the Persian king, gives a theory of the education of a prince and his surroundings, which may deserve a very few words in concluding this chapter.[1] He shares with Plato and Aristotle the belief that private education, with mere prohibitive laws to guide the citizen, is quite insufficient. All the theorists were agreed that there must be one public education, and they imagined that crime would be to a great extent precluded by such effective training.

Xenophon, dividing his period of education into boyhood up to 16, and *youth* (ἐφηβεία) up to 26, provides a regular public school education for the boys, keeping them all together in a sort of polity of their own, where their teaching is performed by special state masters, and

κἂν εἰ πρὸς εὐημερίαν, καὶ διαγωγὴν ἐλευθέραν χρηστέον αὐτῇ· τί γὰρ δεῖ μανθάνειν αὐτούς, ἀλλ' οὐχ ἑτέρων χρωμένων ἀπολαύειν; Σκοπεῖν δ' ἔξεστι τὴν ὑπόληψιν ἣν ἔχομεν περὶ τῶν θεῶν·

οὐ [δὲ] γὰρ ὁ Ζεὺς αὐτὸς ἀείδει καὶ κιθαρίζει τοῖς ποιηταῖς· ἀλλὰ καὶ βαναύσους καλοῦμεν τοὺς τοιούτους, καὶ τὸ πράττειν οὐκ ἀνδρὸς μὴ μεθύοντος ἢ παίζοντος.

[1] The second chapter of his first book gives a general description of the education among the Persians, which is of course a fancy sketch, accommodated to his own theories.

their quarrels and delinquencies settled by tribunals of their own. To the elder youth is assigned all the police and patrol duty, as well as the accompanying of the king in hunting, especially of beasts of prey. This sort of exercise Xenophon had learned to know in the East, and he recognised its superiority over ordinary gymnastics. But the musical education, on which Plato and Aristotle lay such stress, he omits altogether, without giving his reasons. Perhaps he found from experience that the great Aryan nobles were men of refinement, and understood the harmony of life no less than the more theoretical Greeks. He also differs from them in alone recognising the importance of a system which will control not one limited city, but an empire of various peoples and languages. Yet his education is in consequence only the expensive and exclusive training of a dominant aristocracy, and is not supposed to be compulsory for the ordinary citizen. In his State all higher official position is only to be attained by this training.

There are no other ideas in the scheme which make it worthy of any special consideration. The Spartan system blinded the vision of all these speculators, and kept them from understanding the true character of a free and various development of individual genius.

CHAPTER XI.

THE GROWTH OF SYSTEMATIC HIGHER EDUCATION—UNIVERSITY LIFE AT ATHENS.

§ 70. It has been stated in the foregoing chapters that during the earlier or strictly classical period the Greeks never thought of endowing or regulating higher education. The careful system of training at Sparta, promoted and controlled by the State, hardly included even primary education. The police regulations alluded to at Athens only concerned details of management in private schools, and only primary schools, which were worked by masters self-appointed and supported by the demand for them or their popularity in their district. Nowhere do we find anything approaching to a state endowment or regulation of university education. In fact, the want of such higher education was only felt when the Greek mind began to turn inwards upon itself after its extraordinary expansion in the Persian wars. And then the first want was supplied by voluntary efforts, by the Sophists who wandered from town to town, citizens of no fixed state, teachers in complete independence of all state direction. Indeed, their avoidance of political duties and responsibilities often brought them into suspicion, oftener into contempt.

Socrates and Plato brought against them two other objections—the one serious and capital, the other trivial and absurd; and yet it was the latter which told with the public. The former objection was that of superficiality and boastful assumption; they professed within a short time to teach all that was needful in science and literature, in philosophy and in politics. And here the deeper thinking of professed philosophers superseded them, though they had not been either useless or contemptible in their day. The second objection reminds us strongly of the prejudice once felt against taking interest for money—all such profit being regarded as usury in the worst sense of the term. It was urged that the Sophists asked and received pay for spreading the truth, and for teaching what every honest man ought to communicate (if he were able) for nothing. But although it was all very well for the eccentric and exceptional Socrates, for the wealthy Plato, to refuse all remuneration, the theory that the Sophist was not a labourer worthy of his hire asserted that all higher education must be carried on by amateurs, and thus tended to destroy all systematic and widely diffused culture.

§ 71. This narrow prejudice, therefore, did not resist the common sense of the public when brought to bear upon it. We are assured that Plato, like Socrates, took no payment. Our authorities are silent about Aristotle, and it is hence inferred that he followed the same rule. But Speusippus, his successor in the school, is said to have demanded regular fees. This had been the practice with all the rhetoricians who taught young men after their emancipation from school, and who followed the natural precedent of the Sophists. Such a practice was all the more reasonable, as the pupils in philosophical schools, even in Plato's, were divided into amateur pupils, who came for mere general training, and professional students, who meant to take up teaching for their livelihood, and who spent a long time in special studies. Thus pupils' fees were always a possible, and became an actual, endowment for higher teaching. In the Sophists' days men complained that these fees were exorbitant, though perhaps not with justice. In later days we hear of large fees from rich pupils, but always as voluntary donations, and for the purpose of relieving poorer fellow-students. For the schools of philosophy began to be secured from difficulties by a second means of endowment—the donations of patrons and the bequests of pious founders. As regards these donations by rich pupils, we hear from Philostratus[1] that a rich scholar, Damianus, gave to each of the Sophists, Aristeides and Adrianos, 10,000 drachmæ, to supply poor students with free lectures. This gift, about 400*l.* of our money, represents a far larger sum in relation to the then existing conditions of wealth. 100 drachmæ were probably considered an adequate fee for a complete course, and if it be true that a popular teacher could often command 100 pupils, even though the course occupied more than one year, the endowment was considerable.

The desire of procuring free education for poorer lads with literary tastes is, however, an interesting and

[1] Βίοι σοφ. ii. 32, 2.

permanent feature in the Greek mind. At the present moment the University of Athens provides free education for every Greek, and is wholly supported by a state subsidy. This now unique provision brings to Athens an influx of young Greeks from all the Levant, from Turkish countries, from Egypt, nay, even from Italy. They support themselves as best they can, often by menial employments, provided they can keep their lecture hours free. Lodging together in the humblest apartments, they club their scanty earnings for the purchase of a light and a text-book, which they use in common, the one sleeping till his fellow has done his work, and wakes him to hand him the fresh-trimmed lamp and well-worn manual.

This state of things, which reminds us so strongly of the mediæval universities, and is inestimably honourable to a growing age of culture when the masses want leavening, may be driven to a dangerous excess when the educated classes become too numerous, for it dissuades every ambitious young man from agriculture and the commercial pursuits so necessary to a nation's welfare. And as this is the case in Greece now, so it was doubtless the case when in the days of Hellenism Athens offered philosophy at so cheap a rate to all the Greek-speaking world. The class of learned idlers who would not pursue any mercantile calling increased throughout Greece.[1] Although, therefore, the condi-

---

[1] The picture of Athens given in the Acts of the Apostles (cap. xvii.) shows that the city was full of people cultivated in philosophy and letters, but indisposed to pursue any serious calling. They

tion of things at Oxford and Cambridge, which, in addition to their vast endowments, demands a heavy outlay from their alumni, is not to be defended, there is an opposite error, and one likely to do more mischief; it is the setting up of the lower classes to seek university degrees with a minimum of expense and trouble, and consequently a minimum of culture. This mistaken course, which now threatens the Irish people, in addition to all their other misfortunes, tends strongly to increase (as is the case in modern Greece) a dangerous class of social and political malcontents, who consider that their high education is not recognised, and that they have no scope for their literary or political talents.[1]

§ 72. We turn to the endowments by bequest, which were the direct cause of the establishment of philo-

lived in the agora all day, as in a great club, looking out for gossip and news. If anyone desires to see a modern parallel, I refer him to the Hall and Library of the Four Courts in Dublin—the most agreeable place in the world to visit. For there the bar of Ireland, many of them for want of briefs, occupy themselves with all the scandal of the day. Nay, even those who are busy refresh themselves in passing with five minutes' talk, and are never too hurried to enjoy a good story when it is offered to them. There is even a great deal of real business done in this desultory and peripatetic way. Whether a new system of philosophy or a new religion would find a hearing is perhaps doubtful, and marks the difference between the old Greek and the modern idler.

[1] Thus a critic might argue that the present ills of Ireland arise not only from general idleness and want of thrift, but from melancholy ignorance of all scientific principles of agriculture and from a total misappreciation of the conditions of trading, for here if anywhere, honesty is the best policy, but it is not obvious to the ignorant, especially if they be astute. These evils might be diminished by diffusing agricultural and commercial schools through the country, not by granting university degrees for a smattering in arts.

sophical schools at Athens. This idea seems due to Plato, who acquired for his school a local habitation as well as a name. It is well known that from early times there were two *gymnasia* (in the Greek sense) provided for the youth who had finished their schooling—that in the groves of the suburb called after the hero Academus, and that called the Kynosarges, near Mount Lycabettus. The latter was specially open to the sons of citizens by foreign wives. Thirdly, in Pericles' day was established the *Lykeion*, near the river Ilisos. They were all provided with water, shady walks and gardens, and were once among the main beauties of Athens and its neghbourhood.

The Academy became so identified with Plato's teaching, that his pupils Antisthenes (the Cynic) and Aristotle settled beside or in the Kynosarges and Lykeion respectively, and were known by their locality till the pupils of Antisthenes removed to the frescoed portico (stoa) in Athens, and were thence called Stoics. Epicurus taught in his own garden in Athens. All these settlements were copied from Plato's idea. He apparently taught both in the public gymnasium, and in a private possession close beside it; and in his will preserved by Diogenes Laertius, he bequeaths his two pieces of land to Speusippus, thus designating him as his formal successor. His practice being followed, the title *scholarch* soon grew up for the head of the school, and the owner of a life interest in the διατριβή or locality devoted to the purpose. Each master was called the *successor* (διάδοχος) of his predecessor, and the succession of these heads of schools has been traced with more or less success all through the Hellenistic period.

§ 73. This is no doubt the cause of the fixed and traditional character of the philosophical schools at Athens, and one main reason why this city became in the Roman empire, when original research had died out, the principal university of the old world. The successive scholarchs seem to have thought of nothing but the repeating and expounding of the founder's views, and it is mentioned as a special loss to the Peripatetic school, that Aristotle's works were left away from the school, and travelled into the possession of Neleus to Scepsis in the Troad. Hence the scholarchs, instead of developing a new doctrine, were simply helpless, and only taught what they could remember, or what had been preserved by fragments in the notebooks of the school. The proper investment of the school property was also the scholarch's duty, and we hear that in the fourth century A.D., under Proclus, the Platonic endowment was worth more than 1,000 pieces of gold annually. Suidas tells us[1] 'that from time to time pious patrons of learning bequeathed in their wills to the adherents of the school the means of living a life of philosophic leisure.' This is very analogous to the bequests of pious founders in the middle ages, especially of those who had the far-seeing wisdom to free their endowments from the penalty of teaching—a humane and enlightened intention now frustrated by the rage for turning universities into mere training establishments.

'The designating of a successor by will, or shortly

[1] In his Lexicon, sub voc. *Plato*.

before the scholarch's death, became the rule in the principal schools of rhetoric, except that at Athens election by the school came to take its place. So far as we know, this was first suggested by Lycon, Aristotle's third successor, if not by Theophrastus. But the will of Lycon, preserved by Diogenes, is express: 'I bequeath the *peripatos* to my pupils Bulon, Kallinos, &c. without condition. Let them appoint whomsoever they think will be most zealous and best keep together the school. May the rest of the school stand by him for my sake and that of the place.' These words not only imply that there was a staff of assistants, selected from favourite pupils who intended to make philosophy their profession, but is peculiarly interesting as naturally suggesting a competitive examination, without naming it, as the method of choice. In Lucian's *Eunuch*, the appointment is described as an election by votes of the chief men, after an examination of the candidate in his knowledge of, and faith in, the system. There were cases when the electing body was not the school, but the Areopagus, or the council. For the hatred and jealousy of the schools made an election from without safer. When the chief literary posts at Athens became salaried by the State, such interference was natural, and disputed elections were even referred to the Emperor at Rome.

§ 74. Eunapius tells us of an interesting dispute of this kind for the office of *Sophist* (the highest literary post at Athens) on the death of Julianus, 340 A.D., and its consequent vacation. Six candidates—four of them pupils of Julianus, and two other needy persons—were selected by common consent; the Roman proconsul was president of the electing court, and so violent was the canvassing that he was obliged to interfere and order people out of Athens. The candidates handed in essays and made set speeches. There were *claqueurs* ready with their prepared applause. Then the Proconsul again cited them, and gave them a theme for an extempore speech. Five refused, saying they were not accustomed to pour out, but to think out their orations. Prohæresius, a pupil of Julianus, alone took up the challenge, and all applause being interdicted, maintained his reputation splendidly. Nevertheless, he did not then obtain the chair; for his opponents secured influential electors with dinners and presents, and no doubt the social talents of a Sophist in this chair were very important. They took shameful ways of succeeding; 'but indeed,' says Eunapius, 'you can hardly blame them for working their case as best they could.'

This interesting story belongs to later days, when the chairs of philosophy and rhetoric at Athens came under State support and control. In early days, up to the Christian era, the schools were perfectly private, free, and independent of the State. We hear, indeed, of such decrees as that of the thirty tyrants forbidding rhetoric and philosophy to be taught. But though any ancient state, even a free democracy, would have thought itself quite justified in such interference for public reasons, there is no definite attempt at such a policy till the days of Theophrastus, when (about 316 B.C.) Sophocles, son of Amphicleides of Sunium, passed a law that no one should open a school of philosophy without the approval of the senate and people. There was a formal exodus of philosophic students, who only returned with Theophrastus, when Sophocles was convicted under the *law against illegal procedure* (γραφὴ παρανόμων), and his law repealed. This attempt of Sophocles might have been defended from Plato's *Republic* and *Laws*, where the philosopher distinctly recommends State control of education. But it was no doubt the antidemocratic tone of the schools, especially of the Platonic school, which prompted this action, for we hear that Demosthenes' nephew, Demochares, and other democratic leaders, supported Sophocles, on the special ground that Plato's school had supplied most of the later tyrants to Greece.

The true way of controlling education had not yet dawned upon the public men of Athens—the endowing of chairs, with a power of removal. We hear, indeed, gradually of small salaries for *sophronistæ* and other guardians of youth, but direct State patronage of teachers first meets us among the Egyptian and Pergamene successors of Alexander. Then the Roman Emperors, as we shall presently see, appointed regular professors. But all this took the form of honouring a great teacher, as states honoured him with civic freedom, immunity from taxes, bronze statues, and the like. His special teaching was not criticised or directed from without.

§ 75. The time came, however, when more than formal or irregular honours were paid to the teaching profession. The Roman Emperors established chairs (θρόνοι) of theoretical and practical rhetoric, and of the four sects of

Salaries of Professors.

philosophy, the former of which they endowed with 10,000 drachmæ per annum each. The highest chair was entitled the Sophist's Chair, thát term having after all maintained its old respectability, and recovered from the obloquy thrown upon it by Socrates and Plato. There was even a subdivision of the Sophist's chair, a second chair being called the *political* chair. These appointments seem to have been the device of Hadrian, though L. Egnatius Lollianus of Ephesus was the first salaried occupant of the chair, and was appointed under Antoninus Pius. The same policy, carried out by Marcus Aurelius, gave immunity from taxes and civic duties to all the learned professions—physicians, philosophers, rhetoricians, and grammarians. Then the term δημοσιεύειν (*to be a public servant*), once applied to a public hangman or a dispensary doctor, now came to mean a public and salaried professor.

The salaries were paid in kind—five Roman modii of wheat per month—and were thus free from the great fluctuations in money values common in those days. The pupils' fees were paid in money, and were due on January 1, but we hear many complaints of irregularity in this respect. This was mainly caused by the ambition of the rival teachers to have their class-rooms filled, and hence their indulgence in the case of the poor and the procrastinating, who could not or would not pay, and were nevertheless permitted to continue their studies. 100 drachmæ paid down seem to have been thought an average fee; but great variations were allowed, and there was evidently no tariff, or any such credentials as our parchments to show that a man had attended his course, paid his fees regularly, and obtained what we call a degree. Libanius mentions an amusing case of a man sending with his son to Athens a donkey, by the sale of which the fees were to be paid. No doubt the profits made by the greater chairs were considerable, and the *sophist* and *rhetor*, with their higher colleagues, represented Athens on state occasions as civic dignitaries. They were expected to go out to meet any very distinguished visitor, and address him with complimentary harangues; they had to present themselves officially every month to the proconsul at Corinth, presumably to report on the state of Athens. We hear that they obtained leave of absence only by special permission and with difficulty. In contrast to this importance and splendour, we have a pitiable account in Libanius of the miseries of the rhetors at Antioch, who strove to keep up a respectable appearance while they were persecuted with duns and creditors, and almost starved at home.

§ 76. A great deal of obscurity still remains, not only concerning the exact number of salaried professors of sophistic and rhetoric, but concerning their relations to the crowd of assistants, recognised and unrecognised, which must have existed at the university of Athens. So clear was the policy of Hadrian, and still more of M. Aurelius, to make it the main seat of the world's learning, that all manner of students came thither to enjoy the various privileges offered. The grand man, the *Sophist*, could not be expected to do tutor's or coaching work, and as many lads came from the far East and West with little

Appointment of Professors. 143

training, there must have been a considerable class of private teachers to help them on. This was also done by the lad's *pædagogue*, who came with him from home. But there appears to have been a licensed class of secondary professors, the *privat-docenten* of the Germans, who enjoyed no salary, but lived on the fees of pupils. It is not likely that the total number of these licensed lecturers in sophistic and rhetoric exceeded eight or ten; the private tutors were probably very numerous.

We naturally enquire how this State appointment to professorial chairs was consistent with the succession already described in the four philosophical schools. In these there was no formal change; they were elected by a committee of recognised heads of each school. But gradually the influence of the Emperor made itself felt. The procurator, who came from Corinth to look after such matters, either influenced the nomination of the committee, or *recommended* the election of a particular candidate. Even in the case of the public chairs there was sometimes a competition, and often the Emperor did not interfere with his lieutenant's arrangements. Herodes Atticus was almost omnipotent in his day in these appointments. Dismissals from the public chairs were very unusual, but distinctly asserted as the Emperor's right. The Prohæresius above mentioned was dismissed by the Emperor Julian because he appeared to be a Christian.

§ 77. It is more interesting to turn to the peculiarities of life which bound together the young men at the university of Athens, and the various customs which then as now gave a peculiar tone to the student's life. What is called the *atmosphere* of Oxford or Cambridge, of Dublin or Harvard, consists in a body of traditional customs maintained by the peculiar conservatism of youth, which moulds every new comer, and produces a certain type of character, and even a certain fixity of manners. It seems probable that the earliest Italian universities in the middle ages, which go back to the eleventh or twelfth century, acquired some of these traditions from the Greek universities of the decadence, and thus a direct filiation may be traced between the customs now to be described, as existing at Athens in the Hellenistic period, and those of modern Europe. But to investigate this obscure subject thoroughly would lead us far beyond our present limits.

We hear that no one was allowed to attend lectures, at least in the fourth century A.D., without dressing in the scholar's short *cloak* (τρίβων), in fact, our college gown; and the right of wearing it was only obtained by leave of the *Sophist*. This in itself was a mark probably more universal than the gowns at Oxford and Cambridge, for we have no evidence that Greek gentlemen, like the modern English, hated all official costumes.[1]

There was no arrangement for a daily commons of students; there were no college buildings, and the

[1] All foreigners, on the contrary, seem to love official dress, whether military or not. I was once in Genoa during a regatta, when a crew of visitors from Spezia or Livorno used to walk about the streets in boating costume, with their oars over their shoulders, to the admiraion of the Genoese. Imagine the Oxford eight, the day before the University race, sauntering along Piccadilly in this style! I recommend this case to the theorists who maintain that human nature is the same at all times and places.

students lodged where they could, as they do in the foreign universities, such as Göttingen or Leyden. But there were special dining societies in each of the four philosophic schools, meeting once a month or oftener, for which funds were bequeathed, and which were regarded as a special bond of union. Of course, simple fare and philosophical conversation was the original plan; it degenerated into luxury and sumptuous feasting, for the dinners given by Lycon, when head of the Peripatetic school, lasted till the following morning. He entertained twenty at a time for the nominal fee of nine obols, which was even remitted to poor scholars. This took place on the last day of the month. Epicurus in his will made special provision for a feast every 20th of the month. The Stoics had three such clubs, called after scholarchs, who probably were the founders. The intention of these feasts, which were more like Oxford *Gaudies* than ordinary commons, was to bring masters and pupils into closer relation, and this is found a true plan in all modern society. People seldom become intimate who do not dine together.

At Athens, too, there was no official tutorial discipline;[1] there were no compulsory chapels, or lectures, or fines, and order seems to have been kept by the very

[1] The description of Libanius of the rhetor's duty, to receive the lad from his parents, to advise him and even to punish him for idleness, to acquaint the parents periodically of his progress, &c., reminds us perfectly of the duties of a college tutor. But this was clearly a voluntary task, and generally undertaken not merely from duty towards the lad, but from a desire to be popular and to secure a large following.

republican arrangement of a senior prefect (ἄρχων) elected by the class every ten days. We are told that the professor, besides remonstrance, sometimes struck idle or stupid scholars, and Libanius talks of being 'sent down' as a terrible disgrace, involving serious consequences to the lad's parents, and even to his native town. Perhaps it may correspond to expulsion from our universities; but this must have been for the gravest crimes only. The pupils of any professor were merely known as his *circle* (οἱ ἀπό, or περί, τινος); they were only his pupils or hearers in that they attended his lectures. Indeed, they often designated him by a nickname public enough to have been transmitted in after literature.

§ 78. We find an unusual variety of terms,[1] all transferred from other combinations, to express the clubs or unions of students among themselves, and they are constantly mentioned in books and inscriptions of the second and third centuries A.D. They naturally grew out of the old separation of the ephebi into a separate class long before university education was organised, or rather crystallised, into the shape we are now discussing. The presidents of these clubs were called *choregi* (also κορυφαῖοι and ἀκρωμῖται). Inscriptions tell us of similar private combinations among the ephebi in the second century A.D., in which names from the general lists are repeated under the separate heads of *Heracleids* and *Theseids*,

---

[1] Χορός. θίασος, σύνοδος (religious), συνουσία, ποίμνιον, ἀγέλη. I see that Sievers, in his life of Libanius, understands ἄρχων and χόρος of a council of professors, but this is surely incorrect. He was probably misled by finding so much power attributed to a mere student.

two associations to be compared with the students' clubs at the Italian and German universities, which often bear the names of nations, thus pointing to their mediæval origin. There is evidence of some peculiar importance, possibly of rivalry, as regards the Theseids and Heracleids at Athens, and the German critics are probably right in suspecting a political bias to have been the true ground of difference. The constant relations of Heracles and Theseus in the legends and the religion of Attica are well known; the temple of Theseus, still standing at Athens, is by many considered a Heracleion, and the deeds of Heracles are more conspicuously celebrated than those of Theseus in its sculptured reliefs. Theseus was certainly raised by Attic legends into the position of founder of the democracy, and the ideal of an ephebus, and as such he may have been contrasted to Heracles, who was the ancestor of Doric nobility, and might be regarded as of aristocratic tendency. This conjecture has the merit of probability, though it has no basis beyond these general grounds.

§ 79. When we come to later days, especially to the fourth century A.D., we hear much about the students' clubs from Philostratus, Eunapius, Libanius, and others. It is remarkable that they were not then formed on the national basis, as we may conceive the older Heracleids to have been Bœotian youths, severed from the Attic Theseids, or as we could conceive Irish students associating themselves in an English university. They were rather suggested by the rivalries of their teachers, originally of the separate philosophic schools, but afterwards merely formed on the grounds of ambition and popularity. A crowded attendance at lectures was so anxiously desired, that every kind of device was used by the rival professors to induce students to come to them. This evil became so apparent in its effects upon the students, who were flattered and courted by their masters, that Libanius mentions a proposed *agreement* (συνθήκη) between the professors on the question, which was, however, unsuccessful. Thus in the older University of Dublin the profits of college tutors were so great, that a similar rivalry in popularity existed, and the dons are said to have studied unworthy arts to secure a full chamber. Such canvassing has almost disappeared since the *treaty*, as Libanius calls it, of putting the pupils' fees into a common fund, of which the greater part is divided according to the tutor's standing, and only a small premium is allowed for the actual number of pupils.

The constant jealousies and factions occasioned by this competition among professors were reproduced in the Italian universities of the Renaissance period, indeed, all through the Middle Ages. Thus, according to Eunapius, the President of the club called Σπάρτη ἄτακτος considered it part of his duty to bring his club in full force, and well armed, to the Peiræus, or even down to Sunium, in order to catch students coming from the East, green and fresh, and secure them for the professor he patronised. Rival clubs met on these errands, and had pitched battles worse than those of town and gown in England. Every attempt was made to secure lads even before they left their homes. Libanius tells us he came to Athens, having been already canvassed at his home in Antioch to attend the rhetor Aristodemus, but was seized by a club in the interest of Diophantus, and only let free with great difficulty, and after he had sworn allegiance to Diophantus. We hear of every sort of violence being committed by these students, in whose disputes the Roman governor at Corinth was sometimes obliged to interfere. We hear of their debts and their poverty, their dissoluteness and idleness. But of course the diligent and orderly minority have left no trace behind, and we must take care to give no exaggerated weight to the noisy doings of the baser sort. Even tossing in a blanket (or carpet) was well known to them,[1] and applied to unpopular teachers, probably of the obscurer sort, as may be seen from Libanius' oration *on the carpet*, in which he lectures them on the subject. We do not hear of any scholarships, bursaries or exhibitions, intended to help indigent lads of ability. Indeed, this giving a lad money rewards for educating himself seems a very evil device of modern times. To support a student with the bare necessaries of life, and give him free instruction, is a different thing, and this was the idea of the pious founders of scholarships. To repay him in part for an extravagant preparation by extravagant prizes is a very different notion, but now so diffused that its absurdity no longer strikes the public mind in England.

§ 80. Gregory the Nazianzen tells us of comic cere-

[1] Called by the Romans *sagatio*, and hence probably soldiers' horseplay, as *sagum* is a soldier's cloak.

monies by which the freshman was initiated to his studies, and these practices were technically called τελεταί, or initiatory rites. These are to be compared to the teasing of beginners known at the German Universities under the name of *deposition*. At Athens the novice was brought by a band to the baths through the market place. Then those in front began to push him back, and refuse to let him in, while those behind thrust him forward. After a rude struggle, probably intended to try his temper, he was let in, bathed, and thus formally admitted, receiving his *tribon* or college gown. There was also some unknown ceremony in the theatre called κυλίστραι, of which the name only is preserved from its being forbidden by law in 693 A.D., and this by a Church Synod in Constantinople. It was identified with other heathen practices and traditions, and hence considered worthy of being threatened with excommunication. These late occurrences of student practices give rise to the suspicion that they may have been copied in the early school of Bologna. Perhaps the most curious allusion[1] is to the fact, that after a certain standing, students were by common consent excused from these follies, as now in Germany a graduate at Leipzig or Göttingen, or a professor, would no more think of fighting a student's duel than an English gentleman would, while every younger man is compelled to do so by an iron custom, amounting to the most absolute tyranny.

The example of the Stoics, who taught in the city, was followed by other schools, after that the successive

[1] Libanius, i. 17.

devastations of the neighbourhood of Athens by Philip V. of Macedon (200 B.C.), and by Sulla, had injured the gardens and groves of both Kynosarges, Academy and Lykeion. We hear of the *Ptolemeion* and *Diogeneion* as the fashionable places of resort, then Hadrian's gymnasium—all within the town, and all the gift of individual founders, the Diogenes in question being a condottiere who commanded the second King Demetrius' troops in Attica 225 B.C. There is some slight evidence that this man's gymnasium was used for beginners, and possibly they may even have resided there; for we hear that scholars often set up *huts* (καλύβια) near the house of their favourite teachers. There were libraries in connection with Ptolemy's and Hadrian's gymnasia. Indeed, it seems in later days that such was the danger of a riot if professors lectured in any public building, that they built private theatres for themselves, attached to their own houses, and elegantly appointed. In these we may be sure that their teaching took the form of a lecture, not of disputation or of catechising. This latter kind of lesson was very popular in Socrates' and Plato's time, but Aristotle already severed it from his regular discourses, and held his philosophic conversations with his pupils walking in the *Peripatos*: hence the title of his school.

§ 81. We only know now the names of those professors who lived for the world and for posterity, and strove to teach by publishing their works. In an age when originality was dead, and the highest ability consisted in the best commentary on Plato and Aristotle, this literary activity, once admired and praised, seems to us for the most part idle subtlety. Even in rhetoric all the laws and models were fixed ; Longinus only shows us a modern and æsthetic appreciation of beauty in style, which we do not find in earlier rhetors. But of all the scholarchs at Athens none are now of the least consideration save the heads of the neo-Platonic school, and even these were but followers of this strange fascinating doctrine already preached in Alexandria and in Rome, which strove to give a new meaning to the metaphysic of the Academy, and accommodate it to the spiritual wants of earnest heathen, in the face of Christianity.

But it is more than probable that, as in our own Universities, so at Athens, the best and most earnest of the teachers set themselves so exclusively to their task, that they left nothing behind them except in the note books of their classes. This sort of university teacher never earns any wider popularity than that of his college ; and yet there, and among those who have known his diligence, his patience, and his power, he will always rank far higher than those who rush before the public from ambition, often with badly digested ideas. We shall, therefore, do well not to set down the philosophical teaching at Athens at the level of those tedious commentaries which the student will find collected in the later volumes[1] of Mullach's *Fragmenta Philosophorum Græcorum*.

§ 82. As regards the length of the course which the students were expected to attend, there are very varying statements. Five to eight years are mentioned, a period far too long for young gentlemen like Cicero's

[1] ii. and iii. are published ; iv. is to follow.

nephews, and probably only meant to apply to those who went for professional purposes. There were lads of tender age, sometimes under the care of a pædagogue, and men of middle age, waiting for the chance of a post. There seems to have been no limit of age, or any compulsion or rule as to the number of courses to be kept. Every student (or his parent) was supposed to select for himself what subjects he should pursue. This was perhaps less mischievous than it would now be, seeing the quadrivium of humanities was so fixed by tradition that most students fell into it as a matter of course. Neither was there in old days that multitude of special subjects totally unconnected either with each other, or with a liberal education, which now infest our educational establishments, and cause the hurry after tangible results to displace the only true outcome of a higher education—that capacity to think consecutively and clearly which is to be acquired by studying a logical and thoroughly articulated branch of knowledge for the sake of its accuracy and method.

During most of the flourishing age of Hellenistic culture the *rhetor* was the acknowledged practical teacher, and his course, which occupied several years, with the interruption of the summer holidays, comprised first a careful reading of classical authors, both poetical and prose, with explanations and illustrations. This made the student acquainted with the language and literature of Greece. But it was only introductory to the technical study of expression, of eloquence based on these models, and of accurate writing as a collateral branch of this study. When a man had so perfected himself, he was considered fit for public employment. In the latest times a special knowledge of jurisprudence became more and more necessary for public servants, and was provided for by special schools. We have unfortunately no minute description of the precise course of reading adopted by either Sophists or Rhetors, and are, therefore, confined to this general description. But it is, in our days of hurry and of intellectual compression of subjects, a remarkable thing to contemplate the youth of the civilised world spending four or five years in the mere acquiring of accuracy and elegance of expression after they had learned at school reading, writing, and the elements of science.

§ 83. In this account of ancient University life our attention has been almost exclusively confined to Athens, though there were other seats of education very celebrated, and in much request—Rhodes, Massilia, Tarsus, and above all Alexandria. Many Roman nobles preferred sending their sons to Massilia for their education, a Greek town planted far away from the vices and luxuries of the East. Rhodes maintained its political freedom longer than any other Hellenic settlement, and was famous as a school of rhetoric. Tarsus, from which we know at least one splendid specimen of a student—the Apostle Paul—always had a high and solid reputation for work, and it is very remarkable how the most serious of all the practical systems, the Stoic, is identified with that part of Asia Minor. Afterwards iconoclasm found its cradle there, and thus this land of serious reforms over and over again forced upon the world an earnest view of life.[1] It is worthy of note how constantly the great chairs at Athens were filled by men from these outlying schools, indeed a native Athenian in the Sophist's chair was a great rarity. Yet we know so little of the inner life of these remote towns, that they cannot now afford us any materials for our enquiry.

§ 84. The case is different with Alexandria, concerning which much has been written and recorded. But in the first place it is hardly correct to speak of education in Alexandria as strictly Hellenic, or even Hellenistic. It was the meeting ground of all the faith and dogma of the old world. The Egyptian, Jewish, and Syrian elements were so strong there that, considering the absence of all old Hellenic traditions in this newest of all Greek-speaking towns, we could hardly use it as a fair specimen of the good and evil in old Greek training. We may add that up to the days of the great theological controversies — days so graphically pictured in Kingsley's *Hypatia*, we know comparatively little about the students of Alexandria. All our information clusters about the teachers. As we might expect, Alexandria was regarded as the university of progress, the laboratory of positive science in contrast to the conservative and

---

[1] It is said that the exiled iconoclasts, driven out to Bulgaria, were the spiritual parents of the Hussites and other early reformers in Bohemia. From this new centre Protestantism spread across Europe. So that the Scottish Puritan, and for that matter the New England Puritan, derives his uncompromising earnestness from the remote source which produced both Stoicism and the most vigorous early Christianity.

literary Athens. Nevertheless, even all the sound literary criticism of those days comes from Alexandria. For it is plain that the Ptolemies intended it not as a training place for youth, so much as a home for research, richly endowed with the means and materials for serious study, first of all, an ample library, then handsome buildings, retirements, and adequate endowments. These conceptions, and the success in their execution, are profoundly interesting in the history of education, but are beyond the scope of the present work.

www.ingramcontent.com/pod-product-compliance
Lightning Source LLC
Chambersburg PA
CBHW030253170426
43202CB00009B/730